How shall we escape, if we neglect so great salvation; which at the first began to be spoken by the Lord, and was confirmed unto us by them that heard him?

Hebrews 2:3 [KJV]

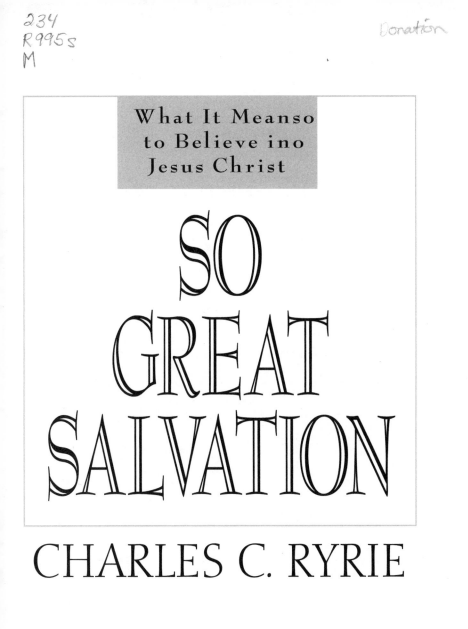

What It Meanso
to Believe ino
Jesus Christ

SO GREAT SALVATION

CHARLES C. RYRIE

MOODY PUBLISHERS
CHICAGO

ISBN-10: 0–8024–7818-2
ISBN-13: 978-0–8024–7818-4

We hope you enjoy this book from Moody Publishers. Our goal is to provide high-quality, thought-provoking books and products that connect truth to your real needs and challenges. For more information on other books and products written and produced from a biblical perspective, go to www.moodypublishers.com or write to:

Moody Publishers
820 N. LaSalle Boulevard
Chicago, IL 60610

5 7 9 10 8 6

Printed in the United States of America

To that group of five, my "elders"
who guard and guide me;

and to
my children,
who love and support me;

and to
a circle of special friends, worldwide,
who encourage and pray for me,

I dedicate this book
with abiding love and gratitude.

CONTENTS

Foreword   9
1. Grace at Camp   13
2. Semantics Alert   19
3. Straw Men   27
4. What Is the Gospel?   35
5. Fruitful or Faithless   41
6. What Is Carnality?   53
7. Of Course He Is Lord   63
8. The Eye of a Needle   73
9. Repent! About What?   81
10. Disciples Come in All Sizes and Shapes   93
11. It's Not Easy to Believe   107
12. The Verdict: Not Guilty   115
13. Secure and Sure of It   125
14. Bringing Many Sons to Glory   135
    Definitions of Key Terms   143
    Scripture Index   147
    Subject Index   153

FOREWORD

I recommend this book to you because of its *subject* and its *object*, both of which are vitally important.

The *subject* is salvation, one of the greatest themes that could ever challenge the mind of man. Confusion about salvation means disaster, for the message of the Gospel is a matter of eternal life or eternal death. "What is the Gospel?" is not an academic question. It affects the destiny of every lost sinner as well as the activity of every witnessing Christian and every soul-winning ministry.

The *object* of this book is assurance. Charles Ryrie helps you to understand what salvation is and how God works this miracle in our lives. He shows us how we can be confident of our salvation and certain that we are forgiven by God and destined for heaven.

This book is not only important, but it is also *dependable*.

To begin with, the author is a theologian who has two earned doctorates in his field of study. He has served effectively on the faculty of one of America's leading evangelical seminaries and is widely recognized and respected as a teacher, preacher, and writer. As you read these pages, you will appreciate Dr. Ryrie's accurate exegesis and his clear explanations of biblical texts.

An experienced and mature scholar, Dr. Ryrie quotes carefully and accurately from a wide range of writers; but his final authority is the Word of God. The cynic Ambrose Bierce once defined "quoting" as "the act of repeating erroneously the words of another." Dr. Ryrie is too seasoned a scholar to make that mistake. You can read these pages with confidence; they are not written by an amateur.

His exceptional knowledge of the Word of God enables Dr. Ryrie to present the subject of salvation in a balanced way. He reminds us that "discipleship" is only one of *many* pictures of the Christian life found in the Bible; he warns us not to divorce it from "all the counsel of God" lest we create serious misunderstandings. He puts matters into their proper perspective as he explains the relationship between faith and works, justification and sanctification, and sonship and discipleship.

Finally, Dr. Ryrie writes with humility and compassion. He has not overreacted to what some extremists have written. Rather, he calmly and logically expounds the Word of God and seeks to bring clarity where there may be confusion, and gentleness where there may be harsh dogmatism. Unlike Gratiano in Shakespeare's *Merchant of Venice*, Dr. Ryrie does not say, "I am Sir Oracle, and when I ope my lips, let no dog bark!" He seeks to obey the words of 2 Timothy 2:24–25: "The Lord's bond-servant must not be quarrelsome, but be kind to all, able to teach, patient when wronged, with gentleness correcting those who are in opposition . . ."

In 1907, when R. J. Campbell published *The New Theology*, the British theologian P. T. Forsyth compared the popular but misleading book to "a bad photograph that was

over-exposed and under-developed." Alas, there are many
"bad photographs" being published these days! That is why I
am especially grateful for a book like *So Great Salvation* that
presents the Gospel "picture" with clarity, accuracy, and maturity; and I pray that God will give it a wide and fruitful
ministry.

–Warren   W.
Wiersbe

But where sin increased, grace abounded all the more.

Romans 5:20

Be kind to one another, tender-hearted, forgiving each other, just as God in Christ also has forgiven you.

Ephesians 4:32

Grace, grace, God's grace,
Grace that will pardon and cleanse within;
Grace, grace, God's grace,
Grace that is greater than all our sin!

Julia H. Johnston

1

GRACE
AT CAMP

Grace is a difficult, perhaps impossible, concept to understand.

In seminary days I had a job working with underprivileged junior-high and high-school kids at the downtown YMCA. On what was then the outskirts of Dallas was a camp we used every Friday night when weather permitted. We would load a bus with forty to fifty kids, head for the camp, and enjoy an evening cookout and games. On special occasions we would sleep there overnight and return Saturday afternoon. Overnight camping trips were usually rewards given to those who had successfully passed certain requirements in our weekly Bible clubs. So the kids who stayed overnight after the others went home were rather special.

One Friday night—or, more accurately, early one Saturday morning—I awoke, startled by some unexplained noise. Soon I discovered that a few of my leaders had sneaked out of the dorm, gone down to the lake, launched one of the boats, and were having a great time far from shore. Not only was this against every rule in the book, but it was dangerous. When the kids knew I knew where they were, they came immediately into shore. Like dogs with tails between their legs, they meekly went back to bed, wondering what punishment awaited them in the morning.

For me, sleep was now impossible. The night before, I had talked to these Christian young people about forgiving one another. So as I paced the grounds in those early-morning hours deliberating their fate, my own words from the night before kept coming back to me, and back to me, and back to me.

If I don't give them some punishment, I argued with myself, *they will never be impressed with the seriousness of what they did. I have a responsibility to the Y to enforce their rules and punish the violators.*

But the more I debated with myself, talked to the Lord, thought about a number of relevant Bible verses (I discovered again that night that you can prove almost anything with a Bible verse), the more Ephesians 4:32 grew larger and larger in my thinking: "Be kind to one another, tender-hearted, forgiving each other, just as God in Christ also has forgiven you."

But, Lord, I can't forgive them; they don't deserve it.
Neither did I.
But, Lord, I have to enforce the rules.
I'm glad, Lord, You didn't.
But, Lord, if I'm too kind, the kids will think I'm weak.
I never thought You were weak, only loving.
But, Lord, first I'll make them promise never to do something like this again, and then I'll forgive them.
It's a good thing You didn't require that of me, or I never would have been forgiven.
. . . just as God forgave me.
How was that? No conditions or promises ahead of time. No works at the time. No remembrance afterward.

But, Lord, You're God—You can do anything.
"You're My child," He said. "Imitate Me."

So with great reluctance and with very little faith, I told the Lord I would.

And then, in the morning, I told the kids.

"You did a terrible thing. It could have had disastrous consequences for yourselves, your families, the Y, and me. But I forgive you unconditionally and completely."

"You're kidding," they said. "There's got to be a catch somewhere."

"No," I insisted, "you are fully forgiven." And then I told them what the Lord had been saying to me that night about His grace, and how I wanted them to have another taste of that grace.

I didn't even make them do the cleaning up that day. I did it myself because I didn't want them to think they could earn even a little bit of that forgiveness.

The rest of the story? As long as those particular kids were in my clubs they were the epitome (as much as kids that age can be) of goodness, helpfulness, and usefulness. They never presumed on that grace.

Grace is indeed a difficult, perhaps impossible, concept to understand.

If it was difficult for those kids to understand an act of grace that forgave one sin on one night, how much more difficult for us to comprehend God's grace that forgives all our sins every day and night, without preconditions, without works, and without remembrance.

We can learn some important matters about grace from this experience.

First, grace is unmerited favor. As a concise definition of grace, this serves well. More elaborate definitions have their place; but simply stated, grace is unmerited favor. It is undeserved on the part of the recipient. It is unearned and unearnable. Those kids had no claim on my grace. They were in a state of total demerit. Anything I might do could not be in response to any merit they had (for they had none at that point) nor as a reward for anything they had done (they only deserved to be punished). My grace that night was pure unmerited favor.

Second, grace is not cheap. Grace is expensive. It is free to the recipient but costly to the donor. The only way one may say that grace is not very costly is if the particular benefit costs the donor very little. My forgiveness that night cost those kids nothing. It cost me a lot of agonizing and soul-searching, which is nothing in comparison with what grace cost our Lord. But to use the word *cheap* in the same breath with the grace of God in salvation seems almost blasphemous. It cost our Lord Jesus His life. Some may insult grace, reject it, trample on it, or disgrace it, but that does not lower its infinite value.

Third, it is not easy to believe someone who offers grace. Those kids were dumbfounded when I announced the verdict of grace. They could not believe what they were hearing. And why should they? From day one they had been reared (and so are we all) in a merit system, in which acceptance is based on performance. "Do this and you will be rewarded. Fail to do this and you will be punished." This kind of merit system permeates all of life and most religions. It is not easy to believe someone who says that he or she will do something good for us that we do not deserve.

Human works are like termites in God's structure of grace. They start small, but, if unchecked, they can bring down the entire structure. And what are such works? Anything I can do to gain any amount of merit, little or much. Water baptism could be one such work if I view it not as an important or even necessary result of being saved, but as a requisite to be saved. It is a work even if I insist that it is God who gives me the desire to want to be baptized that I might be saved.

The same is true for surrender. If surrender is something I must do as a part of believing, then it is a work, and grace has been diluted to the extent to which I actually do surrender.

Fourth, grace that is received changes one's life and be-havior. Those kids, though really not bad before that night, showed a number of changes in their lives. Their bond to me personally was much stronger. They followed me around like puppy dogs anxious to do whatever they could to please me. And they had new insight into the love of their Savior for them.

The Gospel is the good news of the grace of God to give forgiveness and eternal life. Let's keep that Gospel so full of grace that there is no room for anything else to be added to dilute or pollute the true grace of God.

Let the words of my mouth and the meditation of my heart be acceptable in Your sight, O Lord, my rock and my Redeemer.

Psalm 19:14

Be diligent to present yourself approved to God as a workman who does not need to be ashamed, accurately handling the word of truth.

2 Timothy 2:15

2

SEMANTICS
ALERT

A good choice of words is essential if we are to state the Gospel clearly and accurately.

How often I have heard the retort, "It's only a matter of semantics." In my experience it usually came from students using it as a defense mechanism to justify a poor answer to a question. And usually the question involved defining or explaining carefully the meaning of a biblical doctrine or concept. "A matter of semantics" was supposed to excuse fuzzy thinking and a poor, if not wrong, choice of words.

IS SEMANTICS IMPORTANT?

Actually, semantics is not an excuse, nor is it incidental; it is the whole point. Semantics involves the study of meanings of words; so if a person uses words that do not convey the meaning he or she is attempting to express, then a different meaning comes across. If semantics is the study of meanings, then one has to be alert to semantics in all communication.

For example, when an attorney draws up a contract, he or she must pay careful attention to semantics. The choice of words may determine whether or not the contract, if challenged, will remain in force or can be broken. The meaning of the words—semantics—forms the basis for the validity and intention of that contract.

Likewise, Bible students and preachers must pay careful attention to semantics. How carefully they express the meanings of verses, passages, and doctrines will determine the effectiveness and accuracy of communicating God's message to others. (I am not speaking of the matter of differing interpretations. One can hold a wrong interpretation of a passage and yet express it clearly; so too may one have a correct interpretation and express it badly.)

THE PURPOSE OF LANGUAGE

Language was given by God for the purpose of His being able to communicate with man. To be sure, man has corrupted language; but God saw to it that He had sufficient vehicles in languages with which He could communicate to us and we to Him. Although language was confused at the Tower of Babel so that people could no longer understand each other's speech, God nevertheless chose Hebrew, Greek, and Aramaic as sufficient and adequate languages to convey His revelation of truth in the Bible. And, in the other direction, we find English and German and French and any other language on earth adequate to carry our communication in prayer to God.

Christian philosopher Gordon Clark wrote:

> If God created man in His own rational image and endowed him with the power of speech, then a purpose of language, in fact the chief purpose of language, would naturally be the revelation of truth to man and the prayers of man to God. In a theistic philosophy one ought not to say that all language

has been devised in order to describe and discuss the finite objects of our sense-experience. . . . On the contrary, language was devised by God, that is, God created man rational for the purpose of theological expression.[1]

If we acknowledge that language came from God so that He can communicate to us (and we to Him), then semantics, which studies the meanings of words, is crucial if we wish to communicate His truth accurately.

Furthermore, it seems to me that those who believe in the inerrancy of the Bible ought especially to be concerned with accuracy in communicating the truth. All the Bible is without error and important to us. Certainly how we as Christians express the Gospel ought to be our greatest concern. We do not want to confuse or shortchange or obscure God's good news of His grace—how He gave His Son so that we might have eternal life through faith in Him. Semantics is key in understanding and communicating the Gospel.

STATING AND MISSTATING THE GOSPEL

Observe this random sampling of expressions of the Gospel taken from tracts, sermons, books, and radio and TV messages. I list them without documentation since the point is not who said these but to show what was said and to illustrate how varied and confusing these statements are. If we gave even half of them to an unsaved person, which and what would he be expected to believe?

Here they are:

1. Repent, believe, confess your sin to God, and confess Him before man and you will be saved.
2. The clearest statement of the Gospel in the New Testament is found in Luke 9:23: "If anyone wishes to come after Me, he must deny himself, and take up his cross daily and follow Me."
3. Perhaps the most comprehensive invitation to salvation in the Epistles comes in James 4:7–10: "Submit therefore

to God. Resist the devil and he will flee from you. Draw near to God and He will draw near to you. Cleanse your hands, you sinners; and purify your hearts, you double-minded. Be miserable and mourn and weep; let your laughter be turned into mourning and your joy to gloom. Humble yourselves in the presence of the Lord, and He will exalt you "

4. May the Lord reveal to the sinners that the only way for them to be saved from their sins is to repent with a godly sorrow in their hearts to the Lord.

5. Utter the prayer of the Prodigal Son—ask Jesus to be your Lord and Master.

6. Come forward and follow Christ in baptism.

7. Place your hand in the nail-scarred hands of Jesus.

8. Find Christ by praying through to Him.

9. Believe in Him, trust Him, accept Him, commit your life to Him.

10. We have the warning of Christ that He will not receive us into His kingdom until we are ready to give up all, until we are ready to turn from all sin in our lives.

11. God offers eternal life freely to sinners who will surrender to Him in humble, repentant faith.

12. Do we literally have to give away everything we own to become Christians? No, but we do have to be willing to forsake all.

13. Matthew 7:13–14 is pure Gospel: "Enter through the narrow gate. . . ."

14. No one can receive Christ as his Savior while he rejects Him as his Lord.

15. Give your heart to Christ.

16. Ask Jesus to come into your heart.

Not all these statements are incorrect or equally good or bad. But they are not all saying the same thing. They are not expressing the same truth only in different words. The differences cannot be harmonized by saying, "It's only a matter of semantics." And yet they all purport to be explaining the way of salvation.

Just as words were the means God used to record the Gospel in the Scriptures, so words are the means we use to explain the Gospel to others. Therefore, a correct choice of words is important, even essential, in stating the Gospel well.

Notice the different key words in those preceding statements:

> Repent.
> Confess.
> Deny.
> Lord and Master.
> Come forward.
> Baptism.
> Pray through.
> Commit.
> Turn from all sin.
> Surrender.

Some words stand out as poor, even wrong, choices for stating the Gospel. Many would agree that coupling the word *baptism* with the Gospel results in a wrong expression of the Gospel message. But others disagree with this. To them water baptism is a necessary requirement for salvation. For many, faith and works cannot be linked as requirements for salvation. For others, works are involved in becoming a child of God. Whether baptism or works is required in order to be saved is a matter of semantics that in turn becomes a matter of a true or false Gospel.

Most readers of this book will probably agree that *baptism* and *works* are words that should not be used in the Gospel message simply because they mean something that is not a part of the Gospel message. That seems clear enough.

But what about the meaning of a word like *repentance?* That does not seem so clear. Is it part of the Gospel message? Is it a requirement to be saved? Is it only a matter of indifference whether one uses the word or not in presenting the Gospel?

Or what about the word *Lord?* What does it mean if it is made a part of the Gospel message? What about *Messiah? God? Master?*

Or what about the word *give,* as in "Give your heart to Christ"? Is that actually what has to be done if one is going to be saved? Is *give* another way of saying *trust?* And if it is, then is it true that in order to be saved, I must trust my heart to Christ? Or should I say, "Give my life to Christ"?

These are important semantic differences because they give different meanings to the Gospel message. Some give a wrong message; others, an unclear one. But we must strive to use the words that give a clear witness to the grace of God. It is not that God cannot use an unclear message; doubtless He does this more often that He would prefer to. But why should He have to? Why don't we sharpen our understanding of what the Gospel is about so that we can present it as clearly as possible, using the right words to herald the Good News correctly?

Words are crucial. How terribly important they are in statements like these: "Christ died for our sins according to the Scriptures, and . . . He was raised on the third day according to the Scriptures" (1 Corinthians 15:3–4). "These have been written so that you may believe that Jesus is the Christ, the Son of God; and that believing you may have life in His name" (John 20:31).

We shall discuss some of the crucial words in the following chapters with the goal that this will clarify our thinking and then our presentation of God's good news.

NOTE

1. Gordon Clark, "Special Divine Revelation as Rational," *Revelation and the Bible,* ed. by C. F. H. Henry (Grand Rapids: Baker, 1958), 41.

The tongue of the wise uses knowledge rightly.

Proverbs 15:2 NKJV

Let your speech always be with grace.

Colossians 4:6

3

STRAW MEN

Differences of opinion often create straw men. The reason is simple: Straw men are easy to demolish.

According to the dictionary, a straw man is "a weak or imaginary opposition (as an argument or adversary) set up only to be easily confuted."

In the contemporary discussion over the meaning of the Gospel and areas related to it, a number of straw men have been created. In reality these are spurious arguments often raised by proponents of a lordship salvation. Such arguments against those straw men seem more devastating. Realize that a straw man usually is not a total fabrication; it usually contains some truth, but truth that is exaggerated or distorted or incomplete. The truth element in a straw man makes it more difficult to argue against, while the distortion or incompleteness makes it easier to huff and puff and blow the man down.

Throughout this book we will bump against a number of these straw men. But at this point in the discussion it may help to examine some of them in order to clear the air and keep the discussion on realities, not figments.

STRAW MAN #1

The first straw man deals with the role of the intellect and knowledge in salvation. Simply stated, it is: *The Gospel is a sterile set of facts to which we need only give intellectual assent in order to be saved.*

This is the accusation leveled against those who do not hold to so-called lordship/discipleship/mastery salvation. They are accused of teaching that intellectual assent to a set of facts is sufficient for salvation. Sometimes this is labeled "decisional" salvation, for all one needs to do is make an intellectual decision confirmed perhaps by a formula prayer. No one can be saved, says the lordship position, "by a casual acceptance of the facts regarding Jesus Christ."[1]

What makes this a straw man are words like *sterile, intellectual assent,* and *casual.*

Facts are essential. In describing the Gospel he preached, Paul said it was "that Christ died for our sins according to the Scriptures, and that He was buried, and that He was raised on the third day according to the Scriptures" (1 Corinthians 15:3–4). These historical and doctrinal facts are "of first importance" (v. 3), for without them there is no Gospel.

Do these basic facts about the Gospel require only a casual, academic, or intellectual acceptance in order for one to be saved? Not if one defines *faith* as the Greek dictionary does: to "be convinced of something" or to "give credence to." Specifically, to believe in the Gospel is "to put one's trust in" the Gospel.[2] Being convinced of something or putting one's trust in the Gospel could hardly be said to be a casual acceptance of something. When a person gives credence to the historical facts that Christ died and rose from the dead and the doctrinal fact that this was for his sins, he is trusting his eternal destiny to the reliability of those truths.

And that is as far from casual as anything could be.

So you see, the argument erected about the non-lordship view is nothing more than a straw man. With such telling words as *sterile* and *only intellectual assent,* opponents can more easily destroy this straw man. Make no mistake, non-lordship people do not say what straw man #1 alleges they say.

STRAW MAN #2

The second straw man deals with carnality in a believer's life. It is: *A carnal Christian is someone who is saved but who shows nothing of the outworking of his salvation. Or, a true believer can be carnal all of his Christian life and never produce fruit.*

What makes this a straw man are phrases like "shows nothing" or "all of his Christian life." That a Christian can be characterized as carnal cannot be denied, simply because the text of 1 Corinthians 3:1–3 says there were carnal believers at Corinth. Paul addresses these people as "brethren" and "babes in Christ" in verse 1 [NKJV], then he describes them as "men of flesh" and "fleshly" in verses 1 and 3. So there were carnal or fleshly Christians in Paul's day.

What characterizes such Christians? Paul says they walk as mere men (verse 3), that is, like unsaved people. That does not mean that they were in fact not believers; Paul addresses them as believers. But it does indicate that believers may live like unsaved people. To be sure, Christians are not supposed to live like unsaved people, but the reality is that some do.

For how long? More than a moment or a day or a month or a year? When Paul wrote 1 Corinthians, those believers were four or five years old in the faith, and obviously some of them were still carnal or fleshly. Yet Paul expected that by that time they should have matured to the point where he could address them as spiritual.

At this point, one of those "what if" questions will inevitably be asked. What if a true believer seems to live like an unsaved person all of his life? Is he really a believer? Can a believer be carnal all of his life? Or, to phrase it another way, can a believer remain a babe in Christ all his Christian life? If the answer is no, then two options follow. Either such a person was not in fact a believer, or he was and lost that salvation because he did not grow out of spiritual babyhood.

But as long as we are asking "what if" questions, let's ask another. What if one or more of those babes in Christ in Corinth died between the time of conversion and the time Paul wrote 1 Corinthians? In other words, what if a babe in Christ at Corinth died before growing out of that baby state? Did he or she go to heaven? Assuming that such an individual *did* live all his (or her) Christian life in a baby state, if he *is* "in Christ," whether baby or mature, he will certainly be in heaven.

But let's be clear. Even if a believer could be characterized as carnal all of his life, that does not mean that he is carnal in all areas of life. Nor does that mean he will not bear some spiritual fruit during his life. Every believer will bear some fruit. But that is the subject of another chapter.

This straw man eliminates the work, if not the presence, of the Holy Spirit in the life of a believer. As long as the Spirit lives within, no believer can show nothing of the work of salvation and thus be totally carnal all of his life.

STRAW MAN #3

The third straw man concerns the antiquity or recency of a teaching. *If something was taught by the early church, then it must be true. If a teaching is more recent, then its truthfulness is at least suspect, if not untrue.*

Christians can be carnal, living by and for their fleshly desires. We will discuss this more fully in chapter 6. This teaching, however, is said to be new in this century, allegedly making it suspect, if not unbiblical. On the other hand, lordship and lordship-like statements by those who lived earlier in the history of the church must surely indicate that the lordship view is true.

Sometimes this straw man has a mate. Not only does the antiquity of a view make it truthful but also the number of people who held or hold it makes it true. The more the better to substantiate its truthfulness.

Of course, the smoke screen this straw man and its mate throw up can be easily dispelled. The fact that something was taught in the first century does not make it right (unless taught in the canonical Scriptures), and the fact that something was not taught until the nineteenth or twentieth century does not make it wrong, unless, of course, such teaching is clearly unscriptural. Baptismal regeneration was taught in the early centuries, but it is wrong. The majority of the church doesn't practice immersion. Does that make a belief in immersion wrong? Today, the majority of the church is not premillennial (believing in Christ's return for His church before His earthly reign). Does that make that doctrine wrong? The ransom-to-Satan theory regarding Christ's atonement (i.e., that in His death Christ paid a ransom to Satan) was taught in the early church. Does that make it right?

The antiquity or recency of a teaching and the number of people who are for or against it make for interesting study, but neither factor proves or disproves the truth of that teaching.

The charge of newness was leveled against the teachings of the Reformers. With characteristic straightforwardness, John Calvin responded to it this way:

> First, by calling it "new" they do great wrong to God, whose Sacred Word does not deserve to be accused of novelty. . . . That it has lain long unknown and buried is the fault of man's impiety. Now when it is restored to us by God's goodness, its claims to antiquity ought to be admitted at least by right of recovery.[3]

STRAW MAN #4

The fourth straw man underscores the need to represent accurately opposing viewpoints. *Quoting from someone exactly (as indicated by quotation marks around the quote) guarantees an accurate representation of what the person believes.*

That is what proponents of lordship salvation sometimes do when they lift from context quotes by those who hold a position contrary to their own.

It is not difficult to extract a quotation from its context and make it seem to say what you wanted it to say rather than what the author intended it to say and what in fact it *does* say. That kind of straw man is easily demolished, especially if you quote something that seems ridiculous out of context.

The misuse of exact quotations has always made me very wary when writing book reviews. A good book review should evaluate a book from several aspects—what is good about it, what may have been omitted, what the reviewer disagrees with. Relatively few books I have reviewed in my lifetime have been totally and completely bad. Therefore, I try to point out in what areas the book will be helpful. But what often happens is that when the second edition of the book appears, the publisher will redo the dust jacket to include excerpts from published reviews. It goes without saying that the publisher will not publicize any detrimental comments. But in quoting only positive remarks from reviews, the reviewer's evaluation will be misrepresented and sometimes grossly so.

I reviewed a book some years ago and said that it filled "an important gap in our literature," that it "should be studied," and that "The publication of this book will be welcomed by evangelicals." But I also pointed out some of the author's basic presuppositions with which I disagreed and some of his exegesis which I thought to be wrong. What do you think the publisher quoted on the jacket to the second edition?

So be on guard. If for any reason you suspect that a quotation does not fairly represent what you think you know of someone's teaching, then check into it. It goes without saying that to misrepresent intentionally, even if quoting exactly, is unworthy of a Christian author or publisher.

Other straw men, such as using the phrase "cheap grace" or saying that salvation has no practical consequences, will be examined in subsequent chapters. But for now, exposing these four may help clear the air and focus our attention on the meaning of the biblical text about salvation. That's where the truth is, and if we understand it accurately and express it with semantic clarity, both the truth and those to whom we communicate it will be well served.

NOTES

1. John MacArthur, *The Gospel According to Jesus* (Grand Rapids: Zondervan, 1988), 179.

2. Arndt and Gingrich, *A Greek-English Lexicon of the New Testament* (Chicago: Univ. of Chicago, 1957), 666.

3. John Calvin, "Prefatory Address to King Francis," *Institutes of the Christian Religion*, 3.

But the angel said to them, "Do not be afraid; for behold, I bring you good news of great joy which will be for all the people."
Luke 2:10

For I delivered to you as of first importance what I also received, that Christ died for our sins according to the Scriptures, and that He was buried, and that He was raised on the third day according to the Scriptures, and that He appeared . . .
1 Corinthians 15:3–5

4

WHAT IS
THE GOSPEL?

Consider this tale of two students. The first is a straight-A student. He has not received anything less than an A in his entire university career. The second has never received an A in his life. Actually, he struggles to pass.

One semester both find themselves in the same class, and both are in trouble academically. There is a real possibility the A student may receive a B for the course, while the struggling student might not even pass.

The semester ends and both anxiously await their grades. Now suppose the professor goes to the A student and says, "I have good news for you. You passed." To the A student, that is definitely not good news. The only good news he wants to hear is that he received an A. But for the other student, the message that he passed would be the best news he could hear. "You received an A" and "you passed" are both good news, but with quite different content. Both are "gospels," but they are different gospels.

THE GOOD NEWS

Our English word *gospel* means "good story" or "good news."

But the word *gospel* must be further defined by answering one more question: good news about what? Even the New Testament uses the word *gospel* to mean various types of good news, so one has to describe what good news is in view.

For example, in 1 Thessalonians 3:6 Paul wrote that Timothy brought good news, literally a gospel, of the steadfastness of the new converts in Thessalonica. This gospel did not concern eternal salvation; rather it was the good news that the spiritual condition of the Thessalonian believers was vibrant.

Paul warned against the false gospel of the Judaizers in Galatians 1:6. Their good news or gospel included the requirement to be circumcised as well as to believe in order for one to be saved. No gospel of grace was this, for a human work had been added—circumcision.

GOOD NEWS IN THE GOSPELS

In the gospel of Matthew, all but one time the word *gospel* is used concerning the good news or gospel of the kingdom. This was the message of John the Baptist (Matthew 3:1–2), of our Lord (Matthew 4:17), and of the twelve disciples when they were first sent out by the Lord (Matthew 10:5–7).

What was this good news about the kingdom? The correct answer lies in the concept and hope of the kingdom that the Jewish people had at the time of the first coming of Christ. In fact, their hope was for the establishment of the promised rule of Messiah in His kingdom on this earth, and in a kingdom that would exalt the Jewish people and free them from the rule of Rome under which they lived.

But the rule of heaven did not arrive during Jesus' lifetime because the people refused to repent and meet the spiritual conditions for the kingdom. Most only wanted a political deliverance without having to meet any personal requirements for change of life. So the kingdom did not arrive because the people would not prepare properly for it.

But this did not mean there would never be a Davidic, millennial kingdom. The Lord taught that it would not appear immediately (Luke 19:11), but He also predicted that the Gospel, the good news of the kingdom, would be preached yet again in the future period of the Great Tribulation (Matthew 24:14). And in that wicked time when Satan and the forces of evil will have almost totally free rein, it will be very good news to know that soon Messiah will rule on the earth.

All of Matthew's references to the Gospel concern this good news about the kingdom except one, Matthew 26:13. There the Lord said that wherever the good news about His death was preached, Mary Magdalene's good deed of anointing Him in anticipation of that death would be known.

Mark's use of the term *gospel* uniformly emphasizes the person of Christ (Mark 1:1, 14–15; 8:35; 10:29; 13:10; 14:9; 16:15). Our Lord is the central theme of the good news. Luke also used the word to underscore the centrality of Christ to the good news (Luke 2:10) as well as announcing the kingdom (Luke 4:43). John does not use the word *gospel* at all, though of course he records the important teaching on the new birth (John 3:1–21).

GOOD NEWS IN PAUL'S WRITINGS

Paul gives us the precise definition of the Gospel we preach today in 1 Corinthians 15:3–8. The Gospel is the good news about the death and resurrection of Christ. He died and He lives—this is the content of the Gospel. The fact of Christ's burial proves the reality of His death. He did not merely swoon only to be revived later, as some critics claim. He actually died, and died for our sins. The inclusion of a list of witnesses proves the reality of His resurrection. He died for our sins and was buried (the proof of His death); He rose and was seen by many witnesses, the majority of whom were still alive when Paul wrote 1 Corinthians (the proof of His resurrection). This same twofold content of the good news appears again in Romans 4:25: He "was delivered over . . . and was raised." Everyone who believes in that good news is saved, for that truth, and that alone, is the Gospel of the grace of God (1 Corinthians 15:2).

In days past (and even today) we heard much about the "full Gospel," which included experiencing certain ministries of the Holy Spirit. To be saved, one not only had to believe but also, for example, receive the baptism of the Holy Spirit. Churches that taught this doctrine were sometimes called "full Gospel" churches.

Today we hear about the "whole Gospel," which includes the redemption of society along with the redemption of individuals. But Paul wrote clearly that the Gospel that saves is believing that Christ died for our sins and rose from the dead. This is the *complete* Gospel, and so it is also the true full Gospel and the true whole Gospel. Nothing else is needed for the forgiveness of sins and the gift of eternal life.

THE KEY ISSUE IN
UNDERSTANDING THE GOSPEL

Some of the confusion regarding the meaning of the Gospel today may arise from failing to clarify the issues. One is, What is it that bars me from heaven? What is it that prevents my having eternal life? The answer is sin. The second issue is, How can my sins be forgiven? I need some way to resolve that sin problem. And God declares that the death of His Son provides forgiveness of my sin.

"Christ died for our sins"—that's as plain as it could possibly be. Sinners need a Savior. Christ is that Savior and the only valid one. Through faith I receive Him and His forgiveness. Then the sin problem is solved, and I can be fully assured of going to heaven.

I do not need to believe in Christ's second coming in order to be saved. I do not need to receive Him as my present intercessor. But I do need to believe that He died for my sins and rose triumphant over sin and death. I do not need to settle issues that belong to Christian living in order to be saved. I do not need to pledge a portion of my future income in order to be saved. I do not need to be willing to give up smoking in order to be saved.

Matters of carnality, spirituality, fruit-bearing, and backsliding relate to the Christian life, not to the issue of salvation. Only the Lord Jesus, God who became man, could and did resolve that problem by dying for us. He had to be human in order to be able to die, and He had to be God in order for that death to be able to pay for the sins of the world.

Keep the key issue in the Gospel clear: We are sinners and Christ died to provide forgiveness for our sins.

THE DIRECTION OF THE GOSPEL

We also must keep the direction of the Gospel clear.

The good news is that Christ has done something about sin and that He lives today to offer His forgiveness to you and me. The direction is from Christ to me. It is never from me to Him. I do not offer Him anything. How could I? What could I possibly offer that would help meet my need? To offer the years of my life is to offer something very imperfect and something that can do nothing to forgive my sin. To vow my willingness to change is to affirm something I will not consistently keep; and even if I could, it would not remove the guilt of my sin.

Of course, when I receive eternal life from His hand, I bow before an infinitely superior Person. But I bow as one totally unable to do anything about my sin. I bow as a recipient of His grace and never as one who donates anything to Him. In salvation I am always the recipient; the donee, never the donor. If I try to donate anything with respect to becoming a Christian, then I have added a work, and salvation is no longer solely and purely of grace. Keep the direction straight, and keep His grace unmixed with any work.

How blessed is the man who does not walk in the counsel of the wicked, nor stand in the path of sinners, nor sit in the seat of scoffers! But his delight is in the law of the Lord, and in His law he meditates day and night. He will be like a tree firmly planted by streams of water, which yields its fruit in its season and its leaf does not wither; and in whatever he does, he prospers.

Psalm 1:1–3

You did not choose Me, but I chose you, and appointed you that you would go and bear fruit, and that your fruit would remain.

John 15:16

5

FRUITFUL
OR FAITHLESS

Every Christian will bear spiritual fruit. Somewhere, sometime, somehow. Otherwise that person is not a believer. Every born-again individual will be fruitful. Not to be fruitful is to be faithless, without faith, and therefore without salvation.

THREE CAVEATS

Having said that, some caveats, or cautions, are in order.

First, this does not mean that a believer will *always* be fruitful. Certainly we can admit that if there can be hours and days when a believer can be unfruitful, then why may there not also be months and even years when he can be in that same condition? Paul exhorted believers to engage in good works so they would not be unfruitful (Titus 3:14). Peter also exhorted believers to add the qualities of Christian character to their faith lest they be unfruitful (2 Peter 1:8). Obviously, both of those passages indicate that a true believer might be unfruitful. And the simple fact that both Paul and Peter exhort believers to *be* fruitful shows that believers are *not always* fruitful.

Second, this does not mean that a certain person's fruit will necessarily be outwardly evident. Even if I know the person and have some regular contact with him, I still may not see his fruit. Indeed, I might even have legitimate grounds for wondering if he is a believer because I have not seen fruit. His fruit may be very private or erratic, but the fact that I do not see it does not mean it is not there.

Third, my understanding of what fruit is and therefore what I expect others to bear may be faulty and/or incomplete. It is all too easy to have a mental list of spiritual fruit and to conclude that if someone does not produce what is on my list that he or she is not a believer. But the reality is that most lists that we humans devise are too short, too selective, too prejudiced, and often extrabiblical. God likely has a much more accurate and longer list than most of us do.

Nevertheless, every Christian will bear fruit; otherwise he or she is not a true believer. In speaking about the judgment seat of Christ, Paul says unequivocally that every believer will have praise come to him from God (1 Corinthians 4:5).

WHAT ABOUT DEATHBED CONVERSIONS?

Some may wonder, *What about the person who is converted on his deathbed? Will such a person, assuming he or she is truly converted, bear fruit?* If the person dies immediately after receiving Christ, how can he bear fruit? There simply is not time.

Are deathbed conversions an exception to the statement that all believers will bear some fruit? Perhaps not. For one thing, when anyone is converted at whatever stage of life, he experiences peace with God, and peace is a fruit of the Spirit. In some cases, that peace may be seen on the countenance of the dying person. But whether seen by others or not, is it not fruit?

For another thing, our Lord said that when someone is converted there is joy in the presence of the angels of God (Luke 15:10). Would that not be fruit that a converted-on-his-deathbed-and-immediately-dying person bears? Not necessarily fruit to be seen by other people (unless there be some moments just before death when family and friends might see or even hear of the change), but fruit seen and appreciated by angels in heaven. The account of a deathbed conversion may bear fruit in the lives of others soon after the person dies or much later. Reports of this happening at funeral services are not uncommon. So it can truly be said that every believer will bear fruit somewhere (in earth and/or heaven), sometime (regularly and/or irregularly during life), somehow (publicly and/or privately).

Fruit, then, furnishes evidence of saving faith. The evidence may be strong or weak, erratic or regular, visible or not. But a saving, living faith works.

THE THEORY OF RELATIVITY

Those who hold to a lordship/discipleship/mastery salvation viewpoint do not (perhaps it would be more accurate to say "cannot") send an unambiguous message about this matter. On the one hand, they say that the essence of saving faith is "unconditional surrender, a complete resignation of self and absolute submission."[1] True faith, we are told, "starts with humility and reaches fruition in obedience."[2] "Salvation is for those who are willing to forsake everything. . . . Saving faith is a commitment to leave sin and follow Jesus Christ at all costs. Jesus takes no one unwilling to come on those terms."[3] Denying self is essential to salvation: "Eternal life brings immediate death to self. . . . Forsaking oneself for Christ's sake is not an optional step of discipleship subsequent to conversion; it is the *sine qua non* of saving faith."[4]

But what if I do not follow Christ at all costs? What if later on in life I become unwilling to forsake something? Suppose I lack full obedience? What if I take something back that earlier in my experience I had given to Him? How do I quantify the amount of fruit necessary to be sure I truly "believe" in the lordship/mastery sense of the term? Or how do I quantify the amount of defection that can be tolerated without wondering if I have saving faith or if I in fact lost what I formerly had?

The lordship response, in spite of its stringent demands on the nature of what the view calls saving faith, must either say that (1) a disobedient Christian loses his salvation or (2) some leeway exists for disobedience within the Christian life. Since many lordship people hold to the security of the believer, they opt for the latter.

So we read a statement like this: "A moment of failure does not invalidate a disciple's credentials."[5] My immediate reaction to such a statement is to want to ask if two moments would. Or a week of defection, or a month, or a year. Would two years? How serious a failure and for how long before we must conclude that such a person was in fact not saved? Lordship teaching recognizes that "no one will obey perfectly,"[6] but the crucial question is simply how imperfectly can one obey and yet be sure that he "believed" in the lordship/mastery salvation sense? If "salvation requires total transformation"[7] and I do not meet that requirement, then am I not saved? Or if my transformation is less than total at any stage of my Christian life, was I not saved in the first place?

Suppose I was genuinely willing to forsake all when I believed, but later I rejected that willingness or some part of it. How am I to view my salvation? Assuming that willingness was present when I believed, then according to the lordship view, I was truly saved. And if I believe in eternal security, then I cannot lose that salvation. So we are back to a relative amount or degree of disobedience in the Christian life that can be tolerated without doubting the original reception of salvation. A moment of defection, we have been told, is not an invalidation. Or "the true disciple will never turn away completely."[8] Could he turn away almost completely and still be sure he was saved? or 90 percent? or 50 percent? Further, we are told that the motivation that causes us to defect even momentarily makes the difference between proving the reality or falsity of our faith. The motivation of fear, it is said, is permissible, but the motivation of treachery is not.[9]

Frankly, all this relativity would leave me in confusion and uncertainty. Every defection, especially if it continued, would make me unsure of my salvation. Any serious sin or unwillingness would do the same. If I come to a fork in the road of my Christian experience and choose the wrong branch and continue on it, does that mean I was never on the Christian road to begin with? For how long can I be fruitless without having a lordship advocate conclude that I was never really saved?

Consider, too, the possible ramifications of this kind of relativity on mass evangelism, child evangelism, and collegiate evangelism. Should the mass evangelist instruct his counselors to send back to their seats those who are not willing to forsake all in order to be saved?

Should the children's worker attempt to make his young audience face the questions of how they will choose among difficult life-changing options that they cannot even imagine and will not have to face for ten or fifteen years? If, later on, one of those children, now grown, makes a wrong choice, was he or she not saved all those years? Or if we acknowledge that a believer can make a wrong choice, can he make two, or two hundred, and still be saved?

Should the worker on the college campus insist that a collegian who wants to receive Christ hold off until he or she breaks off an immoral relationship? Could such a person be saved at the dorm meeting one evening and yet spend that same night in a continuing adulterous relationship? Or could he or she have two or three days to break off the relationship? Or two weeks or several months? In the meantime, is that person born again?

WHAT ARE BIBLICAL FRUITS?

But back to the biblical teaching on fruit. What is fruit? Actually the question ought to be phrased in the plural: What are fruits that a Christian can bear? The New Testament gives several answers to the question.

First, *a developing Christian character is fruit.* If the goal of the Christian life may be stated as Christlikeness, then surely every trait developed in us that reflects His character must be fruit that is very pleasing to Him. Paul describes the fruit of the Spirit in nine terms in Galatians 5:22–23, and Peter urges the development of seven accompaniments to faith in order that we might be fruitful (2 Peter 1:5–8). Two of these terms are common to both lists: love and self-control. The others are joy, peace, long-suffering, kindness, goodness, faithfulness, meekness, virtue, knowledge, endurance, piety, and brotherly love. To show these character traits is to bear fruit in one's life.

Second, *right character will result in right conduct, and as we live a life of good works we produce fruit* (Colossians 1:10). This goes hand in hand with increasing in the knowledge of God, for as we learn what pleases Him, our fruitful works become more and more conformed to that knowledge. When Paul expressed how torn he was between the two possibilities of either dying and being with Christ or living on in this life, he said that living on would mean fruitful labor or work (Philippians 1:22). This phrase could mean that (1) his work itself was fruit, or (2) fruit would result from his work. In either case, his life and work were fruit. So may ours be.

Third, *those who come to Christ through our witness are fruit.* Paul longed to go to Rome to have some fruit from his ministry there (Romans 1:13), and he characterized the conversion of the household of Stephanas as the firstfruits of Achaia (1 Corinthians 16:15).

Fourth, *we may also bear fruit with our lips by giving praise to God and thankfully confessing His name* (Hebrews 13:15). In other words, our lips bear fruit when we offer thankful acknowledgment to the name of God. And this is something we should do continually.

Fifth, *we bear fruit when we give money.* Paul designated the collection of money for the poorer saints in Jerusalem as fruit (Romans 15:28). Also, when he thanked the Philippians for their financial support of his ministry, he said that their act of giving brought fruit to their account (Philippians 4:17 KJV).

To sum up, fruit includes: (1) a Christlike character, (2) a life characterized by good works, (3) a faithful witness, (4) a pair of lips that praise God, and (5) a generous giving of one's money.

BEARING MORE FRUIT

How can our lives be made more fruitful?

Two answers emerge from our Lord's teaching on fruit-bearing in John 15:1–17. He told His disciples (Judas already having left the group) that He had appointed them to go and bear fruit (verse 16), and in the preceding conversation He told them how to do that.

The two things involved are pruning (verse 2) and abiding (verse 4). Those who are already bearing fruit need pruning in order to bear more fruit, and those who are bearing more fruit need to abide in order to bear much fruit.

PRUNING

First the Lord said that the vinedresser (God the Father) does something to those who are fruitless. Are these people genuine believers or professing believers? Many understand them to be professing believers who outwardly associate with the church but who have never personally received the Savior. Verse 6 would seem to support this view if one believes in eternal security. In other words, since true believers are eternally secure, the branches that are taken away (verse 2) or are cast into the fire (verse 6) must be professing believers since true ones cannot lose their salvation. If one does not believe in security, then these can be true believers who lose their salvation.

But others see fruitless believers as true believers since they are said to be in Christ (verse 2), and since the Lord was talking only to the eleven disciples, Judas having departed the others. If this is the case, then what does the vinedresser do to fruitless Christians? He cuts them off or He lifts them up (the verb may be translated either way, John 1:29, 5:8). If we are to understand that He cuts them off, then this means that He removes them from the earth through physical death. It is a warning similar to the one in verse 6.

If we understand the verb to mean that He lifts fruitless believers up, then the idea is that God encourages the fruitless person to bear fruit by exposing him or her to the sunshine of life.

> To conserve moisture in a dry land, vines were allowed to run on the ground until the blossoms began to appear. It was then necessary for the gardener to lift the vines off the ground so that the blossoms could germinate. Vines were lifted up either on sticks or on stones. The vines thus were put in a place where they could produce fruit.[10]

So if these are fruitless believers, then either the gardener removes them in judgment or, more likely, in my opinion, He lifts them up in blessing and guidance, positioning them so that they can bear fruit.

But what about the branches that *are* bearing fruit? Those He prunes in order that they may bear more fruit. In pruning, the wise and loving vinedresser removes all useless things that would sap the strength of the branch and keep it from bearing more fruit. This may involve removing from our lives unhelpful things, useless things, and harmful things. It could include discipline (Hebrews 12:5–11), physical limitations (2 Corinthians 12:7–10), material losses (Hebrews 10:34), family losses (James 1:27), and unjustified persecution (1 Peter 4:12–16). Whatever it takes, our Father wisely does in order that we may bear more fruit.

These processes of pruning or cleansing (the same word is used in John 15:2–3) come because of the Word of our Lord. The disciples had already experienced this but, like others who would come after them, they would continue to be cleansed. The Word is inseparably linked to pruning and cleansing.

ABIDING

But what about the branches that are bearing more fruit? The Father is not finished or satisfied with them. He longs that they bear much fruit, and the path to that goal is abiding or remaining in Christ (John 15:4–10).

What does it mean to abide in Christ? In simplest terms, it means to keep His commandments. The Lord says that in verse 10, and John reiterates it in 1 John 3:24. Such a definition makes sense, for the more we obey Him the more we remain in Him. When we disobey, we remove rather than remain. The one who keeps God's Word will bear much fruit simply because he is doing God's will as he comes to learn it from the Word.

Abiding brings another benefit: answered prayer (verse 7). Again this makes sense, for the one who keeps God's Word knows how best to pray in the will of God; and, of course, such prayers are answered. Abiding, asking and receiving, and bearing much fruit prove that we are His disciples (verse 8). As far as this passage is concerned, disciples are those who have an intimate relationship and mature experience with the Lord in whom they abide. This discipleship is far more than simply being willing to do God's will; it is doing it and continuing to do it.

Progression marks this passage—no fruit, fruit, more fruit, much fruit. But progression has its opposite: retrogression. Obviously, believers can retrogress from bearing fruit. Very fruitful believers might retrogress to bearing less fruit, and presumably they may even slide back to a fruitless condition for some period of time. And this without losing their salvation or being told that they never had it in the first place. Disobedience to God's commandments would certainly result in retreat just as obedience brings advance. John 15:6 contains a strong warning against disobedience (not abiding in Christ) and the barrenness that results. Such believers lose further opportunities to bear fruit. Their branch withers, and if the barrenness continues unchanged, then at the judgment seat of Christ they will not receive rewards (1 Corinthians 3:15; 2 John 8). (In my opinion the last part of verse 6 refers

to that coming judgment.) At what point in life further opportunities are lost to the disobedient believer the Lord does
not say, but clearly at some point it can happen.

Barrenness and fruitfulness may both be a believer's
experience. And fruit, the Lord said on another occasion, is
produced in varying amounts: thirty-, sixty-, or one hundredfold (Matthew 13:8). If the character traits of 2 Peter
1:5–7 are present, then we will not be unfruitful. If they are
absent, then we *are* unfruitful.

And could not that condition continue for some time?
Remember, even the lordship/discipleship/mastery view acknowledges that it can continue for "a moment." If some
spiritual fruits are present and some absent, then we can indeed be more fruitful at one time and less fruitful at another.
Notice too, according to 2 Peter 1:5, that we supply these
traits in our faith. In other words, faith is already assumed to
be present; then we supply these additional characteristics.
Barrenness does not have to be our experience; fruitfulness,
by the grace of God, can and will be. Every Christian will
bear fruit. Somewhere, sometime, somehow.

NOTES

1. John MacArthur, *The Gospel According to Jesus* (Grand Rapids: Zondervan), 1988, 153.

2. Ibid., 177.

3. Ibid., 78, 87.

4. Ibid., 140, 135.

5. Ibid., 199.

6. Ibid., 174.

7. Ibid., 183.

8. Ibid., 103.

9. Ibid.

10. J. Dwight Pentecost, *The Words and Works of Jesus Christ* (Grand Rapids:
Zondervan, 1981), 144.

But solid food is for the mature, who by constant use have trained themselves to distinguish good from evil.

Hebrews 5:14 NIV

Like newborn babies, long for the pure milk of the word, so that by it you may grow in respect to salvation, if you have tasted the kindness of the Lord.

1 Peter 2:2–3

6

WHAT IS
CARNALITY?

Can a born-again Christian be carnal? Or is carnality something that describes an unsaved person? Or can *carnality* describe both Christian and nonbeliever?

Before discussing these crucial questions, it may help to clear the air on two matters.

Some think that those who teach that Christians can be carnal also must logically conclude that some believers can go through life without ever bearing fruit of any kind. In other words, they think that the teaching about carnality includes the ideas that carnality can be lifelong and so total that carnal believers will never bear any fruit and yet be genuinely saved. But that is not true, for all believers will bear fruit, some thirty-, some sixty-, some one hundredfold (Matthew 13:8). Otherwise, they do not possess the new life.

Those who hold to the teaching that Christians can be carnal sometimes say that the lordship/discipleship/mastery view cannot include any concept of carnality. They reason that if Christ is Lord of life, then logically no carnality can coexist in that life. But obviously, committed Christians—whenever that commitment was made—disobey and become carnal (or rebellious, or backslidden, or whatever you wish to label them). Lordship advocates recognize that. Nevertheless, some who hold to a lordship position prefer to say that, although Christians can do carnal things, there is no such thing as a carnal Christian.

THE MEANING OF CARNALITY

What is carnality? According to the Greek dictionary, the word *carnal* means to have the nature and characteristics of the flesh (or more simply, it means "fleshly"). What, then, is the flesh? In the Scriptures, sometimes it refers to the whole material part of man (1 Corinthians 15:39; Hebrews 5:7), and, based on this meaning, *carnal* sometimes relates to material things like money (Romans 15:27) or to the opposite of our weapons of spiritual warfare (2 Corinthians 10:4). But the word *fleshly* also has a metaphorical sense when it refers to our disposition to sin and to oppose or omit God in our lives. The flesh is characterized by works that include lusts and passions (Galatians 5:19–24; 1 John 2:16); it can enslave (Romans 7:25); and in it is nothing good (Romans 7:18). Based on this meaning of the word *flesh,* to be carnal means to be characterized by things that belong to the unsaved life (Ephesians 2:3).

Do we have at least a tentative answer to the questions posed at the beginning of this chapter? If carnality refers to that disposition or life principle of the unregenerate life, then obviously an unsaved person may be said to be carnal or carnally minded. But cannot believers also exhibit those same traits? If so, then a believer can, under some circumstances, be labeled carnal. If we can first understand what carnality is, then we are in a better position to answer the question, "To whom can the term be applied?"

UNBELIEVERS ARE CARNAL
AND BELIEVERS CAN BE

Do the Scriptures indicate that both unbelievers and believers can be called carnal? I think so.

In Romans 8:5–8 Paul contrasts two kinds of people: those whose mind-sets are according to the flesh (or carnal) and those whose are according to the Spirit. The former group only knows death (now and in the future) whereas the latter knows life and peace (now and in the future). That the former group is unbelievers is clear from Romans 8:9, since only believers have the Holy Spirit. Thus, being "carnal"—that is, living according to the flesh—properly labels unbelievers.

But "carnal" can also describe some believers. How so? Simply because such believers live and act like unsaved people (1 Corinthians 3:1–4). How do we know the people Paul describes in this passage are believers? He addresses them as "brethren" and "infants in Christ" in the first verse.

How do we know they were carnal? He says so three times (verses 1 and 3). In those two verses Paul uses two different words. The word used in verse 1 is *sarkinos* and the one used twice in verse 3 is *sarkikos*. Some see no difference in the meaning of the two words, but others do. If there is a difference, it is this: *Sarkinos* means "made of flesh," that is, weak but without attaching any blame to that condition. In the case of the Corinthians, their weakness was due to their immaturity. On the other hand, *sarkikos* does have an ethical or moral connotation. It means "to be characterized by the flesh, something that is willful and blameworthy." The first word means "made of flesh," while the second means "controlled by the flesh."[1] Notice that Paul does not merely say that Christians "can and do behave in carnal ways";[2] he plainly states, "You are carnal." How then can one charge that "contemporary theologians have fabricated an entire category for this type of person—the 'carnal Christian'"?[3] Obviously, such a designation for some Christians is not a fabrication; it is a scriptural teaching.

This teaching is not found only among contemporary writers. J. B. Lightfoot, commenting on 1 Corinthians 3:1–3, says that *sarkikos* (in verse 3) expresses the moral tendencies, the hankerings of the Corinthians after their conversion.[4] The Dutch theologian Herman Bavinck, in a theology book originally published in 1886, notes that "the Corinthians were washed, sanctified, justified in the name of the Lord Jesus, and by the Spirit of God (1 Cor. 6:11), and were nevertheless carnal (1 Cor. 3:1–4)."[5]

John Calvin recognized the difference between the natural man, the spiritual man, and the carnal man. Of the latter he wrote:

> But he [Paul] does not mean that they were completely carnal, without even a spark of the Spirit of God, but that they were still much too full of the mind of the flesh, so that the flesh prevailed over the Spirit, and, as it were, extinguished His light. Although they were not entirely without grace, yet they had more of the flesh than of the Spirit in their lives, and that is why he calls them carnal. That is plain enough from his adding immediately, that they were "babes in Christ," for they would not have been babes, if they had not been begotten, and this begetting is the work of the Spirit of God.[6]

EVIDENCES OF CARNALITY

What were the evidences of the Corinthians' carnality? In general terms Paul characterizes them as walking or living "like mere men" (1 Corinthians 3:3–4). Certainly other Christian people are not meant, but unsaved people of the world. Paul can only mean that these carnal Corinthians lived like unsaved men. That clarifies why the word *carnal* can label both unbelievers and believers, simply because the lifestyles of both are the same. The cure for the unbeliever's carnality is salvation; the cure for the believer's is to grow in the Lord.

Specifically how does the apostle Paul describe carnality among Christians?

First, he likens carnality to being a babe in Christ. Notice that such people are "in Christ," a designation that makes it clear again that Paul is describing believers, not unsaved people. In other words, carnality can indicate the state of the new believer who is still a weak, immature baby. As I have indicated, the word for *carnal* in verse 1 apparently includes the thought of weakness, which the baby analogy confirms. This person only understands the milk of the Word and cannot take solid teaching, or spiritual meat. Indeed, there would be many areas of biblical truth he does not understand and respond to, and that means he is living in immaturity in some or many aspects of his life.

What would be examples of "milk" and "meat" truth? Lightfoot answers this way:

> Obviously the doctrine of Christ crucified belonged to the former. . . . The best comment on this passage [1 Cor. 3:1–3] is furnished by Heb. v. 11–vi. 2, where the writer, laying down the same distinction between milk and strong meat, describes the former [in the six phrases in 6:1–2]. . . . The doctrine of justification by faith, which, as lying at the foundation of Christian teaching, would fall under the term milk, might still in its more complex aspects be treated as meat, and so it is in the Epistle to the Romans. If it be asked again whether St. Paul is speaking of doctrinal or spiritual truths, our reply is that the two cannot be separated in Christianity.[7]

Second, Paul describes carnality among Christians as continued immaturity beyond what normally might be expected—"You are *still fleshly*" (1 Corinthians 3:3, italics added). The word is slightly different than the one used earlier and contains the thought of willfulness. At Corinth, this willful carnality was characterized by jealousy and strife, including the divisions Paul describes in 1 Corinthians 1:12.

What a contrast such immature behavior is to the spirituality and maturity that come from steady, healthy growth.

HOW LONG?

How long should it take before a believer might be considered spiritual? When Paul wrote 1 Corinthians, the believers were about five years old in the faith, and he expected to be able to address them as spiritual (3:1). But even so, once people are "spiritual" there is further growth to be achieved, more battles to be fought, more knowledge to be acquired, deeper intimacy to be enjoyed.

How long can a believer be willfully carnal or rebellious? Is there a definitive answer to that question? Certainly long enough to produce works of wood, hay, and straw for which he will receive no reward (1 Corinthians 3:12). But somewhere, sometime, he will also do some thing(s) that will merit Christ's praise (1 Corinthians 4:5).

HOW MUCH?

Is this an either/or situation—is one either carnal or spiritual at any given time? Clearly Paul used the label "carnal" of some of the Corinthians without implying they were only partly carnal. Yet we know experientially and from Scripture that flesh and the Spirit battle in the believer, which seems to indicate that there are areas of both carnality and spirituality in the person at the same time (Galatians 5:17). Rather than thinking of varying degrees of carnality and spirituality, perhaps we should think of areas of carnality *and* spirituality as the experience of a growing believer.

HOW SERIOUS?

How serious can the evidences of carnality be in a believer? Is carnality merely a momentary defection? Or a surface, not a serious, thing? To help answer those questions, let's look at some of the sins Peter says believers may commit.

First Peter is addressed to the "elect" (1:2 NKJV) to testify about the "true grace of God" (5:12). When discussing persecution, Peter distinguishes between that which Christians might bring upon themselves by their own wrongdoing and persecution which would result from standing for Christ. If believers are reviled for the name of Christ or if believers suffer because they are Christians, then this glorifies God (4:14, 16).

But between these two verses Peter strongly admonishes his readers never to suffer "as a murderer, or thief, or evildoer, or a troublesome meddler" (verse 15). Does he mean that a believer could be a troublesome meddler? To answer yes seems not too difficult. Does he mean a believer could be an evildoer? Again we can be comfortable with a yes answer. Does he mean a believer could be a thief? Perhaps it becomes a little more difficult to say yes, except we remember that Paul also said believers steal (Ephesians 4:28). But does Peter mean a believer could commit murder? If so, this surely seems to be the depths of carnality. If not, then two choices emerge: (1) either the murderer was a true believer and lost his salvation when he committed the murder, or (2) he was never saved in the first place.

Commentators do not hesitate to acknowledge that believers can be guilty of any of these crimes listed in verse 15. "Peter [encourages] anyone [who bears] any reproach in the name of Christ as a Christian, only not as a murderer, a thief, an evil-doer, or as a busy-body or meddler in other people's affairs."[8] "Here St. Peter must mean 'Take care that no such charge can be brought with truth against you.'"[9] "The Christian must not incur penalties for such deeds, but to suffer for the Name itself is not shameful."[10]

James reminds us that "we all stumble in many ways" (James 3:2). No one, no matter how earnest or how committed, is exempt. When we sin, that is clearly and plainly wrong. When we struggle, it is not necessarily a sign that we are unsaved, uncommitted, or unspiritual.

J. C. Ryle called this struggle for holiness "a good sign," one we should thank God for:

We may take comfort about our souls if we know anything of
an inward fight and conflict. It is the invariable companion
of genuine Christian holiness. . . . Do we find in our heart of
hearts a spiritual struggle? Do we feel anything of the flesh
lusting against the Spirit and the Spirit against the flesh, so
that we cannot do the things that we would? Are we con-
scious of two principles within us, contending for the mastery? Do we feel anything of war in our inward man? Well, let
us thank God for it! It is a good sign. It is strongly probable
evidence of the great work of sanctification. . . . Anything is
better than apathy, stagnation, deadness and indifference.[11]

NOTES

1. Fritz Rienecker, *A Linguistic Key to the Greek New Testament*, ed. by Cleon
   L. Rogers (Grand Rapids: Zondervan, 1976), 392.

2. John MacArthur, *The Gospel According to Jesus* (Grand Rapids: Zondervan, 1988), 129.

3. Ibid.

4. J. B. Lightfoot, *Notes of the Epistles of St. Paul* (London: Macmillan, 1895),
   185.

5. Herman Bavinck, *Our Reasonable Faith* (Grand Rapids: Eerdmans, 1956),
   500.

6. John Calvin, *Corinthians* (Grand Rapids: Eerdmans, 1960), 65.

7. Lightfoot, *Notes*, 185–86.

8. A.T. Robertson, *Epochs in the Life of Simon Peter* (New York: Scribner's,
   1943), 286.

9. G.W. Blenkin, *The First Epistle General of Peter* (Cambridge, England: University Press, 1914), 107.

10. G. J. Polkinghorne, *First Peter, a New Testament Commentary* (Grand
    Rapids: Zondervan, 1969), 596.

11. J. C. Ryle, *Holiness* (London: Hunt, 1899), 82.

Therefore also God highly exalted Him, and bestowed on Him the name which is above every name, so that at the name of Jesus every knee will bow, of those who are in heaven and on earth and under the earth, and that every tongue will confess that Jesus Christ is Lord, to the glory of God the Father.

Philippians 2:9–11

7

OF COURSE
HE IS LORD

Even in English the word *Lord* admits several meanings. Facetiously, a wife might refer to her husband as her "lord and master." In such a phrase the two terms *lord* and *master* are synonymous. Her husband is her master.

If I were to have an audience with, say, an ecclesiastical bishop, I might be briefed to address him as "my lord bishop." *Lord* is simply an honorific title of respect that I would be glad to use. But since I do not belong to the church of which that man is a bishop, I am not acknowledging him as my master in any sense. I take no orders from him. I respect him for his position, and that is the sense in which I would address him as "my lord."

When a circumstance seems inexplicable or entrapping, in our anxiety or helplessness we might cry in desperation, "Lord, help," or in resignation, "The Lord knows."

Either exclamation acknowledges the superiority and perhaps sovereignty of God in that particular circumstance.

A BLEND

When I pray to the Lord, I often and usually unconsciously blend several meanings of the word. I recognize I am praying to a superior. Because I am a believer I acknowledge that superior as God. Usually, but regrettably not always, I realize that He is my master and in control of the matters about which I am praying. I often include the ideas of Friend, Comforter, Guide, and so forth when I pray to the Lord.

Actually you cannot say "lord" or "Lord" without including the meaning of superior or sovereign, even though you personally may have no relation to that lord and to his superiority or rule.

JESUS AS LORD

Of course Jesus is Lord. He is Lord because of who He is. He is also Lord of creation, Lord of history, Lord of salvation, Lord of the church, Lord of disciples, and Lord of the future. But even if there were no creation, no history, no salvation, no church, no disciples, and no future, He was, is, and always will be Lord.

But creation, history, and disciples do exist. How is He Lord to them? He is Lord in various ways and relationships. To the sinful woman He met at Jacob's well in Samaria, He was simply a sir (John 4:11). She called Him lord as a matter of politeness. A centurion called him lord, meaning Rabbi or Sir (Matthew 8:6). Jesus claimed to be the sovereign of the Sabbath (Mark 2:28). To His disciples, He said He was their Lord and Master (John 13:13–16). Thomas ascribed full deity to Jesus when he called Him his Lord and his God (John 20:28). "Lord" can also refer to idols (1 Corinthians 8:5), an owner of an animal (Luke 19:33), or a husband (1 Peter 3:6). Thus the word *Lord* has a variety of meanings and relationships in the New Testament.

LORD IN ROMANS 10:9–10

But what is the meaning of *Lord* in Romans 10:9–10? There Paul writes: "If you confess with your mouth Jesus as Lord, and believe in your heart that God raised Him from the dead, you will be saved; for with the heart a person believes, resulting in righteousness, and with the mouth he confesses, resulting in salvation."

Do these verses mean that one must confess Jesus as Master of his life in order to be saved? Unquestionably, *Lord* means "sovereign," but is Paul saying in the passage that in order to be saved a person must receive Christ as the sovereign of the years of his life on earth? One writer says that "the saviourhood of Christ is actually contingent on obedience to His Lordship."[1] If *contingent* means "dependent on" (as the dictionary indicates), then the statement seems to mean that Christ's being my Savior depends on my obedience to His lordship or mastery over my life.

Another writer, under the heading "Leading Others to Christ," writes,

> Third, there is something for you to do to be saved.
> (1) You must repent . . . Acts 3:19
> (2) You must put your faith in Jesus . . . Eph. 2:8
> (3) You must surrender to Jesus as your Lord (boss) . . .
> Romans 10:9.[2]

Does *Lord* mean "boss" or "master of one's personal life" in the passage? Not according to Everett Harrison, who writes:

> "Jesus is Lord" was the earliest declaration of faith fashioned by the church (Acts 2:36; 1 Cor. 12:3). This great truth was recognized first by God in raising his Son from the dead—an act then acknowledged by the church and one day to be acknowledged by all (Phil. 2:11). . . . Paul's statement in vv. 9, 10 is misunderstood when it is made to support the claim that one cannot be saved unless he makes Jesus the

Lord of his life by a personal commitment. Such a commitment is most important; however, in this passage, Paul is
speaking of the objective lordship of Christ, which is the
very cornerstone for faith, something without which no one
could be saved. Intimately connected as it was with the resurrection, which in turn validated the saving death; it proclaimed something that was true no matter whether or not a
single soul believed it and built his life on it.[3]

Notice Harrison's careful distinction between "objective lordship" and, by implication, "subjective lordship." The
former labels Christ by virtue of who He is, and is true
whether or not anyone ever acknowledges it. The latter relates to that lordship or master relation Christ may have to
the believer, and is true only when someone acknowledges it
to be so for him or her.

William G. T. Shedd, a well-known American Calvinis-
tic theologian, in commenting on the word *Lord* in Romans
10:9, says:

The word *kurios* is the Septuagint rendering of Jehovah, and
any Jew who publicly confessed that Jesus of Nazareth was
"Lord," would be understood to ascribe the divine nature
and attributes to him. It is also the Old Testament term for
the Son of God, and the Messiah; and when Christ himself
asserted that he was the Son of God, and the Messiah, he
was charged with blasphemy (Mat. xxvii. 63–66), and with
equalizing himself with God (John x. 24, 30, 33).[4]

B. F. Westcott, one of the foremost Greek scholars of
the nineteenth century, in commenting on 1 John 4:3, wrote:

To "confess Jesus," which in connection can only mean to
confess "Jesus as Lord" (1 Cor. xii. 3, Rom. x. 9), is to recognize divine sovereignty in One who is truly man, or, in other
words, to recognize the union of the divine and human in
one Person, a truth which finds its only adequate expression
in the fact of the Incarnation.[5]

Two other well-recognized scholars, writing on the meaning of the "word" in Romans 10:8, say: "The subject of the rema [word] which is preached by the Apostles is the person of Christ and the truth of His Resurrection. . . . The power of Christ lies in these two facts . . . His Divine nature and His triumph over death."[6]

Explaining the phrase "Jesus is Lord," the *NIV Study Bible* note says:

> The earliest Christian confession of faith (cf. 1 Co 12:3), probably used at baptisms. In view of the fact that "Lord" (Greek *Kyrios*) is used over 6,000 times in the Septuagint (the Greek translation of the OT) to translate the name of Israel's God (Yahweh), it is clear that Paul, when using the word of Jesus, is ascribing deity to him.[7]

To sum up: Romans 10:9–10 is not dealing with the question of the subjective lordship of Christ, but with His deity and His resurrection. To believe that Jesus (the man) is Lord (God) and that He is alive (which includes the fact that He died) results in righteousness and salvation. Notice too that this interpretation is held by several generations of scholars who represent differing schools of theological thought.

JESUS AS LORD OF MY LIFE

But is Jesus not also to be Lord of my life? Of course He should be, sometimes is, and sometimes is partly so. The cliché "If He is not Lord of all, He is not Lord at all" is simply that—a cliché and not a biblical or theological truth. He can be Lord of aspects of my life while I withhold other areas of my life from His control. Peter illustrated that as clearly as anyone that day on the rooftop when the Lord asked him to kill and eat unclean animals. He said, "By no means, Lord" (Acts 10:14). At that point was Christ Lord of all of Peter? Certainly not. Then must we conclude that He was not Lord at all in relation to Peter's life? I think not.

Dedication is a call to believers. On occasion an individual may face and even settle both the question of salvation and dedication at the same time. Paul apparently did, for on the road to Damascus when he realized that Jesus was alive, he asked, "What shall I do, Lord?" (Acts 22:10). The reply, "Go on into Damascus," of course had nothing to do with salvation but with obedience to the one who had become Paul's Savior.

Actually, it seems that many believers do not settle the matter of the personal, subjective lordship of Christ over the years of their lives until after they have been born again. The New Testament appeals for surrender or dedication are addressed to believers. "I urge you, brethren, . . . to present your bodies" (Romans 12:1). Earlier in the same letter, Paul asked those who had been baptized into Christ (obviously only believers could be described that way) to present themselves to God (Romans 6:3, 13). Those who are indwelt by the Holy Spirit (believers) are exhorted to glorify God in their bodies (1 Corinthians 6:19–20). James too urges his brothers to submit to God (James 4:7). These calls to dedication would be meaningless if it were true that one had to receive Christ as Lord of his life as a part of the requirement for being saved. Saved people need to be dedicated, but dedication is not a requirement for being saved. Neither is willingness to be dedicated an issue in salvation.

SOME QUESTIONS TO THINK ABOUT

Let me ask a few questions that may put these matters of Christ's lordship in better focus.

1. Can I accept Jesus as my Savior without acknowledging Him as the Lord God?
2. Can I accept Jesus as my Savior without acknowledging Him as the Lord/Master of my life?
3. Can I accept Jesus as my Savior without being willing to place my life under His control?
4. Can a dedicated Christian take back part or all of his commitment?

5. If so, does he (or she) lose salvation?

Some of the answers will be addressed in this chapter; others will be answered later.

LORDSHIP, DISCIPLESHIP, AND LUKE 14:16–33

Consider two important sayings of our Lord, spoken one after the other, as recorded in Luke 14:16–33.

The first tells the story of a banquet for which great and elaborate preparation had been made. Many had been invited by the host, and when all the preparations had been completed, a servant was sent to tell those who had been invited that they should now come. But those invited began to make excuses—a real-estate purchase that needed to be seen, oxen that needed to be proved, and a new wife that the husband needed to be with. Remember that the people had been invited ahead of time so that they had ample opportunity to take care of their personal matters during the time the banquet was being prepared.

The host became angry and told his servant to bring in those who were considered inferior (verse 21). Still the banquet room was not filled, so others were invited from the roads and lanes where the poor and vagrants lived (verse 23). (This latter group represents Gentiles who were offered salvation after the Jewish people rejected Christ.)

What clear and repeated displays of the host's grace shine through this parable. He gave three distinct invitations (verses 16, 21, 23), and a reminder to the first group of guests (verse 17). So actually four invitations were issued. In spite of rejection, the host continued to invite people to his banquet. No strings were attached, except to come. No price needed to be paid. No conditions were involved, except to come. Indeed, the host told his servant to compel or persuade (as in Acts 28:19) people to come. He wanted others to enjoy what he had prepared and to enjoy it without cost to them (though at great cost to himself).

But there was a warning that the gracious invitation

would not be renewed, so that those who gave excuses would have no further opportunity (verse 24).

The teaching that follows stands in sharp contrast. Whereas the story of the banquet says "come" and "free," the next says "stop" and "costly." What is free? The invitation to enter the Father's kingdom. What is costly? A certain kind of discipleship.

What kind of discipleship? In this account, discipleship that involved attaching oneself to the Lord, leaving family and possessions to be with Him wherever He went. Discipleship that would involve standing against great opposition.

So the Lord warned the multitudes who were attracted to Him too hastily but halfheartedly that it cost something to be His disciple. It cost (1) supreme loyalty to Him even above family, (2) willingness to die for Him, and (3) literally forsaking everything (not just being willing to do so) to be able to accompany Jesus from place to place. The word *forsake* means "to say farewell" (as in Luke 9:61). One would have to do that at least for the time that he left home to follow Christ. And apparently some had given up possessions and employment in order to hear and learn from our Lord as He and they traveled from place to place.

To emphasize how carefully such a decision should be made, the Lord gave two illustrations: (1) the man who began to build and could not finish because he failed to plan wisely (verses 28–30) and (2) the king who carefully considered the strength of his enemy before deciding whether to fight or sue for peace (verses 31–32). Likewise, the decision to follow (and this meant literally to go from place to place with the Lord) was not to be made lightly, halfheartedly, or hastily.

The contrast between these two sayings of our Lord could scarcely be more vivid.

Come to the banquet. It's free.

Don't rush into discipleship. It's costly.

Today the Lord Jesus, the God-man, offers His feast of salvation freely, and He can do so because He is God who became man. The same Lord Jesus, through many New Testament writers, asks those who have believed to submit to His mastery over their lives. Some do to a great extent. Some do to a lesser extent. No one does it fully and always. But He was, is, and always will be Lord whether He is acknowledged as the God-man Savior or whether He is acknowledged as Master of the believer's life.

He is Lord.

NOTES

1. Marc T. Mueller, "Lordship/Salvation Syllabus," Grace Community Church, 1985, 20.

2. Gene Jorgenson, *Baptist Standard,* 29 March 1986, 13.

3. Everett F. Harrison, "Romans," *The Expositor's Bible Commentary* (Grand Rapids: Zondervan, 1976), 10:112.

4. William G.T. Shedd, *Romans* (New York: Scribner's, 1879), 318.

5. B. F. Westcott, *The Epistles of St. John* (Cambridge: Macmillan, 1892), 142.

6. W. Sanday and A. C. Headlam, *The Epistle to the Romans* (New York: Scribner's, 1895), 290.

7. *NIV Study Bible* (Grand Rapids: Zondervan, 1985), 1721.

Now he who received seed among the thorns is he who hears the word, and the cares of this world and the deceitfulness of riches choke the word, and he becomes unfruitful.

Matthew 13:22 NKJV

8

THE EYE
OF A NEEDLE

He was young, probably early twenties. In the normal course of events he still had most of his life to look forward to.

He also was wealthy. Extremely so. Unlike most who spend years accumulating wealth, he already had more than his share.

He was influential. Already he sat with the Sanhedrin, the governing body of his people.

He was moral. Not many could even begin to claim that they had kept the commandments all their lives. He made that claim.

But deep down this rich young leader knew he lacked the greatest treasure anyone could have—eternal life.

A SAD STORY

The story of his encounter with the Lord Jesus is recorded in Matthew 19:16–30, Mark 10:17–31, and Luke 18:18–30, and a sad story it is.

Recognizing in Jesus a supreme goodness he did not possess, this rich young man asked the Lord what he had to do to gain eternal life.

The question reflected the Jewish perspective of the time. One had to do something great in order to merit eternal life.

Before responding, the Lord probed the young man's concept of Him. In what sense did he call the Lord "good"? Only in the sense that Jesus was a good teacher, but merely a human teacher. That is why the Lord emphasized that only God is good in the intrinsic sense of good. Christ was trying to deepen and widen the man's concept of "good" so that he would acknowledge Jesus as God. Then he might realize that he could not perform anything, no matter how noble, that could grant him eternal life. But Jesus, as God, could, if he would recognize Him for who He is.

However, since the young man did not acknowledge Jesus as God, the Lord answered him from the man's own point of view. If eternal life was to be gained by doing something, then there was no need to ask a new teacher what to do. The law could answer his question.

So Jesus told him to keep the commandments, and he replied that he had done so all his life. Had he really done so? Of course not. No person fails to covet, and no child always honors his or her father and mother. But the young man claimed he had always kept the commandments, and he likely had done so to some degree at least. But no one, including this man, could say he had kept them absolutely.

Let's consider four questions raised by this passage.

WILL OBEYING THE COMMANDMENTS
BRING ETERNAL LIFE?

Question #1 is: *Can one gain eternal life by keeping the commandments, even by keeping them perfectly, if anyone could do that?*

Paul answered that very question at the conclusion of his synagogue message in Antioch in Pisidia. He said that only through Jesus is everyone who believes justified and that no one could be justified by the Law of Moses (Acts 13:39). Later he wrote to the Romans that "by the works of the Law no flesh will be justified in His sight; for through the Law comes the knowledge of sin" (Romans 3:20). So even if the rich young man's claim were true that he had kept the commandments the Lord mentioned, and even if he had kept them perfectly, he still could not have gained eternal life.

In citing the six commandments that He did, our Lord used the Law to try to make the young man face the fact that he was a sinner. This is exactly what Paul said the purpose of the Law was—by the Law comes the knowledge of sin. The man raised the question of gaining eternal life by some meritorious work. He should have raised the question of his own sin and how to have it forgiven, which was what the Lord was trying to get him to acknowledge.

DID JESUS CHANGE THE
NATURE OF THE GOSPEL?

Question #2 is: *Did Jesus introduce here a Gospel different from the one He had previously announced to the harlot at the well in Samaria?* He did not tell her to keep the commandments.

Not at all. She knew full well that she was a sinner. She did not need to be faced with that issue as the rich young ruler did.

But Jesus knew that the man's answer was not entirely true. Even if he had kept all of the commandments specifically mentioned in their dialogue, he had failed to keep some of the other commandments. Obviously he had broken the very first commandment of the Decalogue. He worshiped the god of money as well as the God of Israel (Exodus 20:3). He certainly did not love the Lord with *all* his heart, soul, and might (Deuteronomy 6:5). His love of possessions kept him from that kind of total love for the Lord. Because he apparently did not share his wealth, he also violated the command to love his neighbor as he loved himself (Leviticus 19:18). The proof that you love someone else as you love yourself is that you want to give that person whatever is important or precious to you. How many others of the 613 commands in the Mosaic Law he had failed to keep or violated secretly we do not know. But clearly he had broken at least these.

So the Lord, trying to show the young man his true spiritual and moral condition, told him to sell all that he had and give it to the poor. Then, said the Lord, he would have treasure in heaven.

WILL A VOW OF POVERTY WORK?

Question #3 is: *Can one really gain eternal life by selling all of one's possessions and giving the proceeds to the poor?*

It's easier to dodge this question than to face it squarely. Here is the answer of the lordship/discipleship/mastery salvation position:

> Do we literally have to give away everything we own to become Christians? No, but we do have to be willing to forsake all (Luke 14:33), meaning we cling to nothing that takes precedence over Christ. We must be eager to do whatever he asks. Jesus' request of this man was simply meant to establish whether he was willing to submit to the sovereignty of Jesus over his life.[1]

But unfortunately for the above answer, the verbs in Mark 10:21 are commands: go, sell, give. The Lord did not say: Be willing to go, sell, and give. And in the parallel accounts in Matthew and Luke, imperatives (commands) also are used.

Even though the Lord commanded the man to sell and give, suppose we were to change the question to ask whether we must at least be willing to do something hard, like giving up our possessions, in order to inherit eternal life. An affirmative answer does not match the plain meaning of the words.

If the correct answer to question #3 is yes—we must either give up all or be willing to—then who among your acquaintances has eternal life? Who do you know who is truly and without reservation willing to give up everything for Christ? Would you or I be willing, for example, to die for Christ? I'm personally not sure I could answer unequivocally in the affirmative. Self-preservation is a very strong instinct, and who is to say what any of us might do if faced, as many believers have been, with the prospect of a martyrdom. And yet the Lord said in this same passage that in order to be His disciple one must hate his own life (Luke 14:26).

Of course, no one can ever gain eternal life by giving away his money. So, some say, that is not the point of the encounter (though without question it is what the Lord said to the man). The point, we are told, is that one must be willing to repent of sin and/or commit to the mastery of Christ in order to be saved.

HOW DOES DISCIPLESHIP RELATE TO ETERNAL LIFE?

But suppose the man had been willing to give away all his fortune and even become one of the band who followed Christ. That raises question #4: *Does being a disciple assure eternal life?* Or put another way, Can one be a disciple and not possess eternal life?

Willing disciples sometimes resign their discipleship. Early in our Lord's ministry many did (John 6:66). These were actual disciples of Christ, that is, pupils, which is what the word *disciple* means. But surely one cannot conclude they all had eternal life. Judas furnishes another example of a disciple who evidently did not have eternal life. So do the antichrists in John's day; of these John wrote, "they were not really of us" (1 John 2:19).

Being a disciple—even of Christ—does not guarantee eternal life.

LOVE REACHED OUT BUT WAS REJECTED

The Lord loved this rich young man. Incidentally, the verb used for *love* in Mark 10:21 is *agapao*. As far as we know this man was never saved; therefore, he was one of the nonelect. Observe, then, the Lord loved a nonelect man. His *agapao* love extended beyond the world of the elect. How, then, can the "world" of John 3:16 be limited to the elect, as some say it is?

Our Lord was trying to get the man to admit his unrighteousness, his need of help from outside himself. All the time this leader only asserted his own righteousness by his claim to have kept the commands that the Lord cited to him from the Law. So, unwilling to acknowledge Jesus as God and unwilling to admit his own personal failures and self-centeredness, he went away.

The Lord then applied the lesson for the disciples: It is difficult for anyone who trusts in riches to enter the kingdom. It is not the amount of money that makes it difficult, but the trust in any amount of money. We all tend to trust our strong points or our achievements. It is that trust that often keeps us from seeing our real needs. So was the case with this young man. His strength was in his possessions, and trusting them blinded him from seeing his sin.

HOW DIFFICULT IT IS

How difficult is it for a rich man to enter the kingdom? As difficult as it would be for a camel to go through the eye of a needle, Jesus said (Matthew 19:24; Mark 10:25; Luke 18:25).

A camel was the largest animal in Palestine in those days. The needle was a sewing needle, not a small gate within a larger gate, as is sometimes suggested. No way could a camel with or without its humps squeeze through the eye of a needle. The disciples understood that the Lord was saying that it is impossible for anyone who trusts in riches to enter the kingdom—unless God intervenes and offers a way of salvation that is unrelated to human resources and abilities. The young man did not stay around long enough to hear that message. He would not acknowledge his need of outside help, so he did not receive it. But he could have, for the Lord said that with God all things are possible—even the salvation of this rich young man. But salvation was not on the basis of giving away his wealth.

Possessions make us comfortable. Money focuses our eyes on this world, not the one to come. Being able to have what we want deceives us into thinking we have no needs, especially spiritual ones. We assume that success "obviously" means that God is smiling on us with great favor. It meant that to the Jewish people of Jesus' day; that's what made it inconceivable to them to think that money could actually keep anyone from the kingdom. But it, or anything else that blinds us from acknowledging our sin and need of a Savior, can.

But suppose we do recognize that things cannot give us eternal life. Will giving up those things, or being willing to give them up, then give us salvation? To acknowledge our sins and even to turn from those sins will not gain forgiveness. Only receiving the gift of eternal life from the Savior who died for those sins will.

NOTE

1. John MacArthur, *The Gospel According to Jesus* (Grand Rapids: Zondervan, 1988), 87.

Now [God] commands all people everywhere to repent.

Acts 17:30 NIV

For they themselves report about . . . how you turned to God from idols to serve a living and true God.

1 Thessalonians 1:9

Just as I am, Thou wilt receive,
Wilt welcome, pardon, cleanse, relieve;
Because Thy promise I believe,
O Lamb of God, I come! I come!

−Charlotte Elliott

9

REPENT!
ABOUT WHAT?

Most readers of this book probably are too young to remember the "mourners' bench." I did not grow up in a church that had one, but I knew friends who did. The mourners' bench was simply a place to kneel at the front of the church where the sinner could weep over and confess his sins. Then with a resolve to turn from those sins he would receive Christ as his Savior. Mourning, turning, and believing met at the mourners' bench.

No criticism of this practice is implied. Indeed, it would be a healthy thing to see more sorrow for sin today. But what is the place of sorrow for sin or a resolve to turn from sin in relation to salvation? Since many consider sorrow for sin and repentance to be equivalent, then the questions could be worded, What is the place of repentance in relation to salvation? Must repentance precede faith? Is it a part of

faith or a synonym for it? Can one be saved without repenting? What does it mean to repent?

GENERIC MEANINGS

A number of scriptural terms have a basic, almost
generic meaning yet require that one ask some questions in
order to understand the exact meaning in a particular situation. For example, the word *salvation* means "to rescue or to
save." But you must ask a further question about this basic
meaning if you are to understand the meaning in a particular
context: To be rescued from what? In Philippians 1:19 (KJV)
Paul uses the word *salvation* to mean rescue from his con-
finement in Rome. In that text, salvation does not mean rescue from eternal damnation but deliverance from his present
incarceration. But, of course, in other contexts salvation does
refer to being rescued from eternal condemnation (Acts
4:12). Yet the basic meaning of salvation remains the same
whether it refers to a temporal or an eternal rescuing.

Or another example. What does it mean to *redeem?* It
means "to buy or purchase something." To purchase what,
one must ask, in order to tailor this generic meaning to its
use in a particular passage? In Matthew 13:44 a man re-
deems a field; that is, he buys it. This use has no relation to
the redemption our Lord made on the cross, though the
same word is used of the payment He made for sin when He
died (2 Peter 2:1). The basic meaning remains the same—to
purchase—whether the word refers to paying the price for a
field or for sin.

The same principle applies to the word *repentance.* In
both the Old and New Testaments *repentance* means "to
change one's mind." But the question must be asked, About
what do you change your mind? Answering that question will
focus the basic meaning on the particular change involved.

Back to the mourners' bench. Many people conscious-
ly or unconsciously connect repentance with sorrow, so
much so that sorrow becomes for all practical purposes the
meaning of repentance. Sorrow may well be involved in a re-

pentance, but the biblical meaning of repentance is to change one's mind, not to be sorry. The presence or absence of sorrow does not necessarily prove or disprove the genuineness of the repentance. The change of mind, however, must be genuine and not superficial.

Biblical repentance also involves changing one's mind in a way that affects some change in the person. Repentance is not merely an intellectual assent to something; it also includes a resultant change, usually in actions.

HOW THE NEW TESTAMENT
USES REPENTANCE

The New Testament usage of *repentance* can be separated into three categories. First, *there can be a repentance that either has no relation to eternal salvation or at least does not result in salvation.* This may be labeled nonsaving repentance. It is not superficial, and it has a result or effect, though not salvation.

Here is a nonbiblical example of nonsaving repentance: "Guilty," the judge declares. "Guilty of driving while under the influence of alcohol. You must serve ten days in jail in order to learn the seriousness of your actions." So the person goes to jail. Let's suppose this sentence was passed on a white-collar, upper-middle-class person. A jail experience would be especially traumatic for such an individual. So during those ten days he has time to think seriously about his behavior. And during those days there is genuine repentance. It may or may not be accompanied by tears. But in either case it is not superficial. Resolutions are made, and when he is released, he goes through a program that helps rid him of the craving for alcohol.

Or take another example that involves an equally genuine repentance but with an altogether different resultant action. Now the "convict" is a shoplifter. He too is repentant (that is, he has a change of mind) but not about the crime of shoplifting, rather about the faulty method that resulted in his being caught. In this case, the repentance focuses on method, and the result will be to change the method of shoplifting the next time around.

R. C. Trench, in his classic, *Synonyms of the New Testament,* cites a passage from Plutarch in which two murderers who, having spared a child, afterward repented *(metenoesan)* and tried to slay it. He also cites another instance in which *metameleia* (another word for repent, also used in the New Testament) is used in the same sense of repenting of something good to do something bad.[1] Notice that both these examples involved a change of mind about something good, not about sin. *After* the repentance, sinful things were done.

The first-century Jewish historian Josephus used this same concept of repentance. Concerning Herod's fear of the power of John the Baptist he wrote:

> Accordingly he [Herod] thought the best course was to arrest him [John the Baptist] and put him to death before he caused a riot, rather than wait until a revolt broke out and then have to repent of permitting such trouble to arise. Because of this suspicion on Herod's part, John was sent in chains to the fortress of Machaerus . . . and there put to death.[2]

The Bible also gives examples of genuine but nonsaving repentance. Do you remember the story Jesus told about two sons (Matthew 21:28–32)? One said he would do his father's bidding, but did not. The other said he would not, but afterward repented and obeyed. His repentance had nothing to do with salvation. It resulted in his going to work in his father's vineyard. No superficial repentance, but it nevertheless was nonsaving.

Judas, who betrayed our Lord, repented after he learned that the authorities had condemned Him and returned the thirty pieces of silver that had been given him. Though it was genuine repentance, it did not save Judas.

After he had bargained away his birthright, Esau tried to retrieve it without success. The writer of Hebrews states that Esau could not find repentance though he sought it (whether the repentance or the restoration of the blessing) with tears (12:17). Had he been able to repent, it would have resulted not in eternal salvation but in receiving the blessings of his birthright. It would have been a nonsaving repentance.

The conclusion: The presence and experience of repentance do not necessarily result in everlasting life or even in a change for the better.

Second, *there is a repentance that is unto eternal salvation.* What kind of repentance saves? Not a sorrow for sins or even a sorrow that results in a cleaning up of one's life. People who reform have repented; that is, they have changed their minds about their past lives, but that kind of repentance, albeit genuine, does not of itself save them. The only kind of repentance that saves is a change of mind about Jesus Christ. People can weep; people can resolve to turn from their past sins; but those things in themselves cannot save. The only kind of repentance that saves anyone, anywhere, anytime is a change of mind about Jesus Christ. The sense of sin and sorrow because of sin may stir up a person's mind or conscience so that he or she realizes the need for a Savior, but if there is no change of mind about Jesus Christ there will be no salvation.

The clearest use of the word *repent* in this saving sense is found in Peter's sermon on the Day of Pentecost (Acts 2:38). We often get so tied up in some of the other parts of that verse—the question of baptism or the reception of the Holy Spirit—that we miss the significance of "repent."

Some in the Pentecost crowd, hearing Peter's plea to repent, may have wondered, *What do you mean, Peter? Repent about what?* If they listened closely—and if we recall what Peter's sermon was all about—the answer to that question is clear. The apostle first had spoken about Jesus of Nazareth: His life, His death, and His resurrection (Acts 2:22–24). Next, quoting from Psalm 16:8–11, Peter had reminded his audience that Messiah would be raised from the dead, and that since David himself was dead and buried, he could not have been speaking of himself but of Messiah (verses 25–31). Then the apostle made it extremely clear that Jesus of Nazareth, who had risen from the dead less than two months before in that very city, was Messiah. Furthermore, since David also predicted (in Psalm 110) that Messiah would ascend to the right hand of God and since David himself had not ascended but Jesus of Nazareth did (as proved by His sending the Holy Spirit), then Jesus must be the Messiah or Christ.

In other words, Peter painted two pictures—one of Messiah from the Old Testament, highlighting His resurrection and His ascension, and the other of Jesus of Nazareth, who did rise from the dead and did ascend into heaven.

Now the inescapable conclusion: Jesus is both Lord or God, and Christ or Messiah (verse 36). A Jewish audience had the greatest difficulty acknowledging these two claims for Jesus. To assert that the man Jesus was God and also Israel's Messiah and to ask the people to believe that was an almost insurmountable obstacle.

That the noun *Lord (kurios)* refers to God or Yahweh seems quite clear from the other occurrences of *kurios* in Peter's message. Notice verses 21, 34, and 39, where Peter says that the *kurios* is "our God." Full deity, not mastery or discipleship, was the issue.

On the significance of this phrase, "made Him both Lord and Christ," F. F. Bruce wrote: "The foundation truth on which the Church was built. The first Christian sermon culminates in the first Christian 'creed': cf. *kurios Iesous* [Lord Jesus] (Rom. x. 9; 1 Cor. xii. 3). . . . *[Kurios]* represents the Ineffable Name of God (cf. ver. 21)."[3]

Upon hearing and realizing this, conviction overwhelmed the people. They asked what they should do, and Peter replied, "Repent." Repent about what? Change your minds about Jesus of Nazareth. Whatever you thought about Him before or whoever you thought He was, change your minds and now believe that He is God and your Messiah who died and who rose from the dead. *That* repentance saves.

Indeed, before any of us came to Christ we had some conception of Him. Perhaps it was fuzzy, perhaps it was reasonably clear, perhaps it was wrong. But we turned from whatever conception we had and turned to Him as our Savior from sin. And that repentance brought eternal salvation.

An interesting sidelight—"repent" in Acts 2:38 is a command. We repent. We do it. And yet God gives repentance (Acts 11:18). This is analogous to believing. "Believe" is a command (Acts 16:31). We do it. It is truly our faith (Romans 4:5, "his faith is credited as righteousness," i.e., the faith of the one who believes is counted for righteousness). And yet the whole of salvation, including faith, is the gift of God (Ephesians 2:8–9).

The lordship/discipleship/mastery teaching apparently makes repentance and faith two distinct and necessary requirements for salvation. Note, for example, this statement:

> The demand is for repentance as well as faith. It is not enough to believe that only through Christ and His death are sinners justified and accepted. . . . Knowledge of the gospel, and orthodox belief of it, is no substitute for repentance. . . . Where there is . . . no realistic recognition of the real claims that Christ makes, there can be no repentance, and therefore no salvation.[4]

However, Luke's rendering of the Great Commission uses repentance in the same sense as believing in Christ. "And He said to them, 'Thus it is written, that the Christ would suffer and rise again from the dead the third day, and that repentance for forgiveness of sins would be proclaimed in His name to all the nations, beginning from Jerusalem'" (Luke 24:46–47). Clearly, repentance for the forgiveness of sins is connected to the death and resurrection of Christ. Other passages where repentance stands for faith and refers to the conversion experience are Acts 5:31; 11:18; Hebrews 6:6; and 2 Peter 3:9.

Paul said that God calls on all people everywhere to re-

pent because judgment is coming and the Person God raised
from the dead will be the judge (Acts 17:30–31). Peter said
the same thing. God is long-suffering, not willing that any
should perish but that all should come to repentance. Does
this mean just to be sorry for sin? Does this mean that repentance is a precondition to faith? No to both questions. If repentance is not a synonym for faith in these verses, then
these verses do not state the Gospel. If repentance is only
part of conversion (faith being the other part), then these
verses state only a half Gospel.

It is striking to remember that the Gospel According to
John, the gospel of belief, does not use the word *repent* even
once. And yet John surely had many opportunities to use it in
the events of our Lord's life which he recorded. It would have
been most appropriate to use *repent* or *repentance* in the account of the Lord's conversation with Nicodemus. But *believe* is the word used (John 3:12, 15). So if Nicodemus
needed to repent, *believe* must be a synonym; else how could
the Lord have failed to use the word *repent* when talking with
him? To the Samaritan harlot, Christ did not say repent. He
told her to ask (John 4:10), and when her testimony and the
Lord's spread to other Samaritans, John recorded not that
they repented but that they believed (verses 39, 41–42). And
there are about fifty more occurrences of *believe* or *faith* in
the gospel of John, but not one use of *repent.* The climax is
John 20:31: "These have been written so that you may believe . . . and that believing you may have life in His name."

But, some may ask, *what about Acts 20:21?* Summariz-
ing his ministry in Ephesus, Paul said he testified to both
Jews and Greeks of repentance toward God and faith in
Christ. Does this not show that *repentance* and *faith* are not
synonymous? Or at least that repentance is a precondition to
faith? No, because the two words, *repentance* and *faith,* are
joined by one article which indicates that the two are insepa-
rable, though each focuses on a facet of the single requirement for salvation. Repentance focuses on changing one's
mind about his former conception of God and disbelief in

God and Christ; while faith in Christ, of course, focuses on receiving Him as personal Savior.

It has also been suggested that in this summary Paul is emphasizing the distinction between the particular needs of Gentiles and Jews. Gentiles who were polytheistic needed to change their minds about their polytheism and realize that only one true God exists. Jews needed to change their minds about Jesus and realize that He is their true Messiah.

Certainly when one changes his mind about Christ and receives Him as Savior, changes will follow in his life. All believers will bear fruit, so changes will follow.

A third category of uses of the word *repent* concerns repentance within the experience of Christian living. Christians need to repent. Recall the man at Corinth who sinned and who, exercised by the church's discipline, came back to the Lord. Apparently the church was overly harsh on him, not being willing to restore him to full fellowship (2 Corinthians 2:5–8). Thus Paul exhorted the church to repent of its harsh stand and receive the man again into fellowship. *Repent* in this instance means that the church should change its mind about its wrong attitude toward that man.

In 2 Timothy 2:25 Paul commands Christians, or at least professing Christians, to repent of sin in their lives, particularly sins connected with promoting and accepting false teachers.

In the letters to the seven churches in Asia Minor is a cluster of exhortations to Christians to repent. Ephesians were warned to repent over their loss of first love (Revelation 2:5); those in Thyatira, of their immorality (2:21–22); those in Sardis, of their deadness (3:3); and the Laodiceans of their lukewarmness (3:19). So clearly individual Christians and local churches need to repent about any number of sins.

THE MAIN POINT

To return to the main point of this chapter: Is repentance a condition for receiving eternal life? Yes, if it is repentance or changing one's mind about Jesus Christ. No, if it means to be sorry for sin or even to resolve to turn from sin, for these things *will not save*. Is repentance of sin a precondition to faith? No, though a sense of sin and the desire to turn from it may be used by the Spirit to direct someone to the Savior and His salvation. Repentance may prepare the way for faith, but it is faith that saves, not repentance (unless repentance is understood as a synonym for faith or changing one's mind about Christ). Our Lord came to seek and to save those who are lost (Luke 19:10) simply because those who are healthy do not need a physician; only those who are sick do (Matthew 9:12).

Should one preach repentance today? Of course, but keep the meaning clear. Perhaps calling on people to repent—that is, to be sorry for their sins—will make them realize that they need some way to have those sins forgiven. Perhaps repentance will create a longing for ridding oneself of bad habits. The Spirit can use repentance as sorrow to direct some to the Savior, who forgives and gives new life. But sorrow alone cannot save.

To preach repentance in the sense of changing one's mind about Jesus Christ is basic, for without that kind of repentance no one will be saved. However, in the New Testament, faith serves as a synonym for that kind of repentance. So emphasize faith as well. That is the emphasis from the gospel of John on through the New Testament epistles.

Certainly, Christians need to repent. This is an aspect of repentance we seem to give little emphasis to today. We Christians do need to change our minds not only about specific sins but also about things that we often refuse to acknowledge as sins. Such repentance will include confessing those sins, which will in turn bring restoration to fellowship with our Father and His family. Remember too that local churches need to repent of sins that are just as common today as they were in first-century churches.

Urge repentance. But always make it clear about what.

NOTES

1. R. C. Trench, *Synonyms of the New Testament* (London: Paul, 1886), 259.

2. Josephus, *Antiquities,* XVIII, 116–19.

3. F. F. Bruce, *The Acts of the Apostles* (Chicago: InterVarsity, 1952), 96.

4. J. I. Packer, *Evangelism and the Sovereignty of God* (Downers Grove, Ill: InterVarsity, 1961), 72–73.

If you abide in Me, and My words abide in you, ask whatever you wish, and it will be done for you. By this is My Father glorified, that you bear much fruit, and so prove to be My disciples.

John 15:7–8

10

DISCIPLES COME IN ALL SIZES AND SHAPES

The Great Commission recorded in Matthew 28:18–20 commands us to make disciples. This involves two activities —baptizing and teaching. Baptizing is a single act; teaching is a continuous process. Disciples have to be baptized (an evidence of salvation—therefore, one may say that disciples must first be saved); then they have to be taught over and over to obey (observe all things).

In New Testament times, baptism served as one of the clearest proofs that a person had accepted Christ. Baptism was not entered into casually or routinely as is often the case today. Although it is clear in the New Testament that baptism does not save, to be baptized was to signify in no uncertain terms that one had received Christ and was also associating himself with the Christian group, the church. Of course, there may have been exceptions; i.e., there may have been some who were baptized who had not been born again. But normally, a baptized person was a saved person; and a saved person was a baptized person. This is why our Lord's Great Commission can use "baptism" as equivalent to "salvation."

An important observation: A baptized person (a saved person) can genuinely be saved and yet not be taught, at least not very much. Teaching must follow, but it cannot be made a prerequisite or even a necessary part of receiving Christ.

Certainly, a deathbed convert who dies immediately or almost so will not be taught and thus will not fulfill the second part of the Great Commission. Is such a person not truly saved because he never had time to show he was a disciple? Indeed, such an individual would most likely not even be baptized. I think one would have to conclude that a deathbed convert, though genuinely saved, does not meet the description of a disciple as being both baptized and taught according to the Great Commission.

Although three verb participles surround the imperative "make disciples" in the commission, the first verb is correctly translated as an imperative "go." This same construction is found in Matthew 2:8 where the same word *go* in a participial form must be translated as an imperative.

The commission commands us to make disciples who are saved, learning, and obeying disciples. But disciples do not always come in that shape.

VARIETY OF DISCIPLES

The word *disciple* itself means "learner or pupil." It always involves a teacher-student relationship. John the Baptist had his disciples (Matthew 9:14), the Pharisees had theirs (Matthew 22:16), and Paul had his (Acts 9:25).

Our Lord had many (Luke 6:17). Some learned only for a time, then defected and left Him (John 6:66). On Palm Sunday a multitude of disciples followed the Lord, but by the end of the week most of them had also defected (Luke 19:37–39). Some were believers (John 8:31). One at least, Joseph of Arimathea, was a secret disciple for some time (John 19:38). A few belonged to an inner circle of intimate friends (Matthew 10:1; 17:1). Our Lord expected discipleship to involve strict commitment (Luke 14:25–33). But that does not always happen in the lives of all disciples.

So disciples come in all shapes and spiritual conditions.

The word *disciple* never appears in the New Testament outside the Gospels and the book of Acts. This may be because a disciple was expected to physically follow his teacher wherever he went, and this meant leaving his family and occupation so as to be able to be with that teacher all the time. After Christ's resurrection and ascension, this aspect of discipleship (of Christ) was impossible (go and make disciples. . .), so the word was used less frequently in the book of Acts and not at all in the remainder of the New Testament.

Great Commission disciples are believers who are learning and obeying. But learning and obeying are not *prerequisites* for believing; they are *products of* believing. If the examples of disciples in the Gospels may be carried over into today, then we would have to conclude that there are some disciples who learn a little, some a lot; some who are totally committed, some who are not; some who are secret, some who are visible; some who persevere, some who defect. But all are believers (or at least professing believers who have been baptized).

No disciple will fail to learn something (unless he be a deathbed convert). But how much he will learn, no one can say. No disciple will fail to bear fruit, but how much and how visible and how long, no one can say. Neither can anyone place quantitative requirements on learning or fruitfulness in order to prove the reality of the discipleship.

Consider Joseph of Arimathea. After Jesus' death, he went to Pilate to request the Lord's body in order to prepare it for burial and to place it in the tomb he had for his own eventual use. John says that he was a secret disciple of Jesus because he feared the Jews (John 19:38). Yet the Gospel writers say clearly that he was a disciple of Jesus. How long had he been a disciple before our Lord's crucifixion? We do not know for sure. But for some length of time Joseph had been both a member of the Sanhedrin (Luke 23:50) and a secret disciple of Jesus. He did not consent to the Sanhedrin's decision to condemn Jesus, but that did not necessarily unmask him and reveal him as a follower of Jesus. He may simply have removed himself from the deliberations. Even when he asked permission to have the body of Jesus, his secret was not revealed to everybody.

If a proponent of lordship/discipleship/mastery salvation had been living in the days of our Lord, and if he had been asked at any time before the trial and crucifixion of Jesus whether Joseph was one of His disciples, what do you suppose would have been his unhesitating answer? "No, this man was not a disciple."

ACTS 16:31: A CALL TO LORDSHIP?

Today, the discipleship concept of Teacher-student in the Gospels has been transferred to a Lord-servant relationship. We are being told that one cannot be a true believer unless he has surrendered to the mastery of Christ over his life. We are told that a person must take Christ's yoke when he believes or he is not a true believer. Again we are told that there is no salvation apart from cross-bearing. Or, in order to be saved, "You must accept Christ as your Savior and your Master."

Thus, for example, Paul's response to the Philippian jailer's questions about how to be saved in Acts 16:31—"Believe in the Lord Jesus Christ"—is understood to mean believe in Jesus' death and lordship (i.e., mastery) over one's life.

Incidentally, why is it that those who teach that you cannot receive Jesus without receiving His personal mastery over the years of one's life do not also insist that we must receive Him as Messiah (the meaning of *Christ*) with all that the concept of Messiah entails? That would mean, for starters, that in order to be saved one must believe that Jesus is Israel's promised deliverer, the one who fulfills many Old Testament prophecies, and the one who is the coming King over this earth. Is the acknowledgment of all that Messiah means part of the necessary content of faith for a genuine salvation experience?

Let's suppose that *Lord* in a verse like Acts 16:31 means Master over one's life and that this is a necessary requirement for salvation, along with faith. Then are we to understand that a person cannot be truly born again without deciding the issue of mastery over life? If so, then how much mastery? Must all the areas of his life be yielded at the point of conversion? Must one submit to the mastery of Christ or at the very least be willing to do so in order to be saved? Many say yes loudly and passionately.

But, of course, we must find our answer from the Bible. What light does it throw on this very important and serious matter that is at the heart of the Gospel message?

In some, the motive for insisting that mastery be a part of the Gospel may be an attempt to ensure that converts will "pan out." This is certainly a worthy motive, for all of us are concerned about the dropouts among those who profess to believe. But adding another requirement to the Gospel will not cure this, for many who might make this mastery commitment would not keep it. And if they do not keep it, perhaps it was not a genuine commitment in the first place and thus not a genuine conversion.

Simply stated, the question is: Does the lack of commitment to the mastery of Christ over the years of one's life mean there can be no saving faith? Is faith without mastery saving faith?

The question is not whether believers will sin, or whether they will bear fruit. They *will* sin, and they *will* bear fruit. Nor is the question whether believers should face the matter of who will direct the years of their lives. The question is whether commitment of life (or the willingness to do so) is a necessary part of faith and thus of the Gospel.

As Gentry wrote, "The lordship view expressly states the necessity of acknowledging Christ as the Lord and Master of one's life in the act of receiving Him as Savior. These

are not two different, sequential acts (or successive steps),
but rather one act of pure, trusting faith."[1] And Pink has argued, "Something more than 'believing' is necessary to salvation. . . . No one can receive Christ as his Savior while he
rejects Him as Lord!"[2]

SOME FAVORITE SALVATION VERSES

Some of the favorite New Testament verses about salvation do not include the requirement of submission, but
only faith. John 1:12 promises that those who receive Him
will become children of God. The "Him" is, of course, Jesus,
but in the context the emphasis is placed on Jesus as God,
not Master of lives. He is the Word (verse 1); He is God
(verse 1); He is the Creator (verses 3, 10); He is life and light
(verse 4); He was incarnated (verse 14); He replaced the
Law of Moses (verse 17); and He was the One who made
God known (verse 18).

The emphasis in John 1:1–18 seems to be that we must
receive Him who is God and who became man. It is the
God-man Savior whom John asks us to receive. Nowhere is
the matter of personal lordship or mastery over one's life in-
troduced.

The lordship/discipleship/mastery position explains John
1:12 this way: "John 1:11–12 contrasts those who 'received'
Him with those who rejected Him as Messiah. Those who received Christ were people who embraced Him and all His
claims without reservation."[3] But the only claim in this passage seems to be the claim that He is the Messiah. That is not
a mastery claim, but if it is the claim that people must em-
brace without reservation, one would think that almost all
Gentiles who say they are saved are in fact not. Not many
Gentiles face the messianic claims of Christ when they receive Him.

Neither does the oft-quoted John 3:16 introduce or include or even imply that the mastery question is part and
parcel of the requirement to believe. The Lord stressed to
Nicodemus that He was the one who descended from heaven

and that He was the Son of Man. So, again, the emphasis as far as the person of Christ is concerned was on His being both God and man. Whoever believes in that unique, only begotten person will have eternal life.

The lordship/discipleship/mastery position declares that this verse "means more than accepting and affirming the truth of who He is—God in human flesh—and believing what He says."[4] What more? That writer's next sentence is, "Real faith results in obedience."[5] No one will debate that, because believers will bear fruit. But to inject the issue of mastery over one's life into John 3:16 as a condition for "real faith" rather than a consequence is to add something the verse does not say.

Of course, one has to be willing to come to such a person, but the issue of mastery over life is not involved in receiving the gift of eternal life. It is very much involved in God's desire for His children, but facing and deciding that issue does not bring us into the family of God.

The illustration from the Old Testament in John 3:14 does not support the lordship/discipleship/mastery position. The mastery issue was not involved when the Israelites were told to look at the serpent on the pole in order to be healed of otherwise fatal snakebites (Numbers 21:4–9). They only had to look to live. They did not have to commit to be willing to follow God through the rest of their wilderness experiences. And indeed they did not follow Him thereafter. They may not have complained again about the food they had to eat, but they did sin again very grievously when they worshiped Baal of Peor (Numbers 25:1–3).

Look and live! Some who looked must have just been bitten. But they saw around them those dead from the bites. Others must have themselves been near death. How long a look? A glance or a minute? How close to the pole? Just within sight or near enough to touch? With sickened, glazed eyes or clear eyes? Those things made no difference. To look was all that was required for healing.

The Hebrew word for *look* used in Numbers 21:8

"calls for no special comment, for it is the common word for seeing with the eyes."[6] A different root for *look* in Numbers 21:9 "represents that which one does with the eye (Ps. 94:9), embracing everything from a mere glance (1 Sam. 17:42) to a careful, sustained, and favorable contemplation (Isa. 5:12; Ps. 74:20; 119:6, 15). It is frequently paralleled to *ra'a* 'to see' [the word used in verse 8]."[7] So the particular words used in this passage convey no special significance to the kind of look an Israelite had to give. Regarding what was required for deliverance, one commentator has noted:

> Had the serpents been merely removed, according to the prayer of the people, yet that would not have healed the wounded. A remedy was to be provided that should also recover the dying, and save the living. . . . The believing Israelite hears, even in his dying agonies, the proclamation of deliverance, lifts up his drooping head, looks, and is healed. . . . It was solely by a look that the effect was produced. There was nothing else required [of] the bitten Israelites. . . . They were simply to look upon the serpent as God's ordinance for recovery.[8]

Another favorite salvation verse is John 5:24: "Truly, truly, I say to you, he who hears My word, and believes Him who sent Me, has eternal life, and does not come into judgment, but has passed out of death into life." Here faith is to be directed toward God, who sent Christ as the Son of Man.

Again, the emphasis is on the Son of Man who came from heaven. No issue of mastery is raised in this promise. The same holds true for John 6:40: "For this is the will of My Father, that everyone who beholds the Son and believes in Him will have eternal life." No issue of mastery is included—only believe in the Son whom the Father sent.

If mastery is a requirement for being saved, then are these favorite salvation verses incomplete, misleading, or just plain wrong?

THE SAMARITAN WOMAN
AND THE NEED TO MASTER SIN

Or what about the Samaritan woman with whom the Lord conversed at Jacob's well? What requirements did He lay on her? She had five husbands or men that she had lived with, and the one with whom she was living was not her husband (John 4:18). Plainly, she was living in sin. What an opportunity for the Lord to inject the matter of willingness to leave that immoral relationship in order to have living water (eternal life). What a great case study this woman could have been for all mastery advocates from that time to this. But He had already told her what was necessary for her to have living water (John 4:10)—to know the gift (not reward) of God, and who He was, then ask Him for that water.

Even after some of the details of her sordid past and present came to light, Jesus did not change His message. He did allow her to sidetrack Him with her question about where to worship, but He led that part of the dialogue back to the fact that He was the promised Messiah (verse 26). The Bible does not tell us whether or not the woman left her live-in man and mended her ways, but the record is crystal clear as to how she could have eternal life. People receive the gift of eternal life by asking Christ for it.

EXAMPLES OF UNCOMMITTED BELIEVERS

The Bible also records clear examples of people who were saved but who lacked, or even refused, commitment.

Remember Lot. He scarcely qualifies as an example of commitment at any point in his life as it is recorded for us. It would be difficult to point to fruit in Lot's life. He seemed never to repent of much of anything. He was selfish. He so lacked character that he offered his two virgin daughters to the men of Sodom in order to spare his two guests (Genesis 19:5–8). His testimony was of little value to either his own family or his in-laws, for they turned a deaf ear to his warning of impending judgment. Even Lot himself was reluctant to leave Sodom and had to be dragged away from it (Genesis 13:11; 19:14, 16). Yet the New Testament declares he was a righteous person (2 Peter 2:7). If the requirements of mastery salvation were applied to him we would have to conclude he was not saved. But the New Testament says he was.

Think about the condition of the believers at Ephesus (Acts 19:1–20). Paul ministered in that city more than two years. Some believed at the beginning of his ministry; others, later on. They were converted from a lifestyle that included devotion to magical arts based on the gibberish that was written on the statue of Diana in the great temple at Ephesus. But even after believing in the Lord, many, perhaps most, of those believers (and Acts 19:18 clearly states that they *were* believers) still continued their superstitious practices. It would be wishful thinking to imagine that they did not know such practices were wrong when they accepted Christ and during those two ensuing years when they continued to do them.

The books of magical arts were directly linked to the idol in the temple. But not until the end of Paul's ministry in Ephesus did the believers finally become convicted about these sinful practices, confess their sins, and burn the books. Clearly, there were people at Ephesus who became believers in Christ knowing full well that they should give up their use of superstitious magical arts but who were unwilling to do so (some for two or more years), but who nevertheless were born again. Their salvation did not depend on faith plus submission to the mastery of Christ in relation to their sinful use of magic. Even their unwillingness to give up those books did not prevent their becoming new creations in Christ. Their salvation did not depend on faith plus giving up or being willing to give up their belief in superstitious practices.

At any time during those few years, lordship advocates (had they lived back in those days and visited in the homes of some of those believers) might have looked at the lives of such Ephesians and concluded they were not saved. But the Bible says they were. So who are we to impose conditions on them (to at least be willing to give up their books of magical arts) or on anyone? God does not; we must not.

There are many commands to be obeyed by Christians, but to become a Christian only requires receiving the gift of eternal life from our Lord.

"CAN HE NOT BE SAVED?"

Some years ago in another country, I was literally accosted after an evening service by a group of American missionaries working in that country. They had been infected by the lordship/discipleship/mastery Gospel, and having read the thirteen pages I had written about the subject in 1969, they were anxious to debate the issue. I did not know them; they were uninvited; but I could not avoid meeting with them. So we talked for quite a while that night.

Finally it came down to an illustration. I posed this case to them. We all knew, even at that time, that smoking had been proven a serious risk to one's health. I asked about a hypothetical person who wanted to be saved, but he smoked. Furthermore, he knew full well that smoking was endangering his health, and he realized that if he became a Christian he ought to give it up. But he was unable to do so, nor was he even willing. So I asked these folks, "Can he not be saved until either he gives up smoking or is willing to give up smoking?" Reluctantly they admitted that their view compelled them to say no, he cannot.

Now, suppose such a person made a profession of faith that, as far as one could tell, was genuine. Could he truly be saved and continue to smoke, knowing that is a clear violation of God's desire that we take care of our bodies? If he continued to smoke till the day of his death, would I be forced to conclude that his profession was not genuine and that he had not been saved all that time? Or could I be assured that in spite of that area of initial unwillingness when he came to Christ and continued disobedience while he lived the Christian life, he nevertheless would be in heaven? The answer is a resounding yes.

These are important matters for all of us to consider carefully as we seek to clearly present God's good news.

NOTES

1. K. L. Gentry, "The Great Option: A Study of the Lordship Controversy," *Baptist Reformation Review* 5 (Spring 1976): 52.

2. Arthur W. Pink, *Present-Day Evangelism* (Swengel, Pa.: Bible Truth Depot, n.d.), 14.

3. John MacArthur, *The Gospel According to Jesus* (Grand Rapids: Zondervan, 1988), 106, n.

4. Ibid., 46.

5. Ibid.

6. R. Laird Harris, Gleason Archer, and Bruce Waltke, *Theological Wordbook of the Old Testament,* vol. 2 (Chicago: Moody, 1980), 823.

7. Ibid., 546.

8. George Bush, *Notes, Critical and Practical, on the Book of Numbers* (New York: Ivison & Phinney, 1858), 315–17.

For the Scripture says, "Whoever believes in Him will not be disappointed."

Romans 10:11

I know not how this saving faith
To me He did impart,
Nor how believing in His Word
Wrought peace within my heart.

But "I know whom I have believed,
And am persuaded that He is able
To keep that which I've committed
Unto Him against that day."

Daniel W. Whittle

11

IT'S NOT
EASY TO BELIEVE

There ought to be a law. A law against a merchant accepting a personal check in payment for anything under twenty dollars.

How often I have waited and waited in line while someone writes a check to pay for six dollars' worth of groceries or eight dollars' worth of miscellaneous items.

Why the wait? Simply because it is not easy to believe.

Imagine you are the customer trying to cash the check. You know the check is good. And perhaps even the cashier has received your checks from you earlier and knows you're good for the amount. It doesn't matter. The scenario is always the same. "Let me see your driver's license." Then she has to punch in the number to be sure your record is clear. All clear. "Let me see a major credit card." She punches in that number. All clear. At last the clerk initials the check. Now the store believes you. But it wasn't easy.

We're only talking about money. And most of the time not a very large amount.

BELIEVING IN JESUS IS NOT EASY

Suppose the issue was not six or eight dollars but eternal life? And suppose I was being told that to have eternal life all I had to do was believe. It would not be easy to believe. Too much is at stake, and the more that is at stake, the harder it is to believe.

When we Christians ask someone to believe in the Lord Jesus Christ, we are asking something very difficult. We are asking the person to believe in someone he or she has never seen. Someone who lived in the very distant past. Someone who has no living eyewitnesses who can vouch for His character and the truth of His words. Someone whose biography was written very long ago and by those who were His friends.

For another reason, we are asking someone to believe in an almost unbelievable concept when we ask him to believe that Christ can forgive his sins. The issue at stake is not the tab at the supermarket or whether someone lived and said this or that. We are asking the person to believe that this unseen individual, Jesus, who lived so long ago, can forgive sins, give eternal life, and guarantee us a home in heaven. And this forgiveness can be given because He died as our substitute. Is this easy?

If one's faith is mistaken or misplaced, it could be a very costly error. The issue does not concern a few dollars or a few years of life on earth. It concerns eternity. Since all of this is involved in faith, it is not easy to believe.

WE BELIEVE ALL THE TIME

And yet we all do believe in hundreds of ways every day. We believe that everyone at the water company is doing his job well, so we can turn on the tap and drink safely. We believe that the letter we mailed will be delivered. We believe that the skill of engineers and contractors who designed and built the many buildings we walk in and out of will keep them from falling on our heads. And (this one always amazes me) we believe the cashier who tells us, "Your photos will be back in one hour."

WHAT IS FAITH?

What is faith? Is it merely assent to facts? Does it involve any kind of commitment, particularly the commitment of the years of one's life on earth? What does it mean when the Bible says that the demons believe and shudder (James 2:19)? How can some people apparently believe and not be saved, while others believe and are saved?

Faith means "confidence, trust, holding something as true." Certainly, faith must have some content. There must be confidence *about* something or *in* someone. To believe in Christ for salvation means to have confidence that He can remove the guilt of sin and give eternal life. It means to believe that He can solve the problem of sin, which is what keeps a person out of heaven.

One can also believe Christ about a multitude of other things, but these are not involved in salvation. A person can believe He is Israel's Messiah, and He is. One can believe He was born without a human father being involved in the act of conception, and that is true. A person can believe that what Jesus taught while on earth was good, noble, and true, and it was. He can believe Jesus will return to earth, and He will. One can believe Christ is the Judge of all, and He is. A person can believe He is a prophet and a priest, that priesthood being shaped after the order of Melchizedek, and one would be right.

We can believe all those things. You and I also may believe He is able to run our lives—and He surely is able to do that, and He wants to. But these are not the issues of salvation.

The only issue is whether or not you believe that His death paid for all your sin and that by believing in Him you can have forgiveness and eternal life.

Faith has an intellectual facet to it. The essential facts are that Christ died for our sins and rose from the dead (1 Corinthians 15:3–4; Romans 4:25). In addition, faith involves assent or agreement with those facts. One can know the facts of the Gospel and either agree or disagree with them. But faith also involves an act of the will, for we can decide either to obey or to reject God's command to believe (Acts 16:31). And making whichever choice we do involves our will.

These three aspects of faith are quite standard in theology. For example, Charles Hodge summarized the meaning of faith that is connected with the Gospel this way:

> That faith, therefore, which is connected with salvation includes knowledge, that is a perception of the truth and its qualities; assent, or the persuasion of the truth of the object of faith; and trust, or reliance. The exercise, or state of mind expressed by the word *faith*, as used in the Scriptures, is not mere assent, or mere trust; it is the intelligent perception, reception, and reliance on the truth, as revealed in the Gospel.[1]

Please observe the clear focus of Hodge's definition. He is defining faith "which is connected with salvation."

Louis Berkhof, a Reformed theologian like Hodge, included the same three elements in faith: (1) an intellectual element *(notitia)* or knowledge; (2) an emotional element *(assensus)* or assent to the truth; and (3) a volitional element *(fiducia)* or the involvement of the human will.[2]

In elaborating on the third element in faith—the volitional —Berkhof focused clearly on what that consists of. He wrote: "The third element consists in a personal trust in Christ as Saviour and Lord, including a surrender of the soul as guilty and defiled to Christ, and a reception and appropriation of Christ as the source of pardon and spiritual life."[3] And further, "The object of special faith, then, is Jesus Christ and the promise of salvation through Him. The special act of faith consists in receiving Christ and resting on Him as He is presented in the gospel."[4] Berkhof did not speak to the issue of the mastery of Christ over one's life when discussing these three elements of faith. His third aspect, *fiducia,* concerned the involvement of the human will in personal trust in the Lord for salvation, not commitment of the years of one's life to His mastery (contrary to the proponents of lordship salvation).[5]

John Murray, another Reformed theologian, also saw the same three elements in faith: *knowledge, conviction,* and *trust* are his words. In further describing trust, he wrote it is

> A transference of reliance upon ourselves and all human resources to reliance upon Christ alone for salvation. It is a receiving and resting upon him. It is here that the most characteristic act of faith appears; it is engagement of person to person, the engagement of the sinner as lost to the person of the Saviour able and willing to save. . . . Faith is trust in a person, the person of Christ, the Son of God and Saviour of the lost. It is entrustment of ourselves to him. It is not simply believing him; it is believing in him and on him.[6]

MORE THAN FACTS

From these suggested descriptions of faith, it is obvious that faith involves more than the knowledge of facts. The facts must be there or faith is empty. But even assent, however genuine, must be accompanied by an act of the will to trust in the truth that one has come to know and assented to.

Hodge's use of the word *trust* may be particularly appropriate today, for the words *believe* and *faith* sometimes seem to be watered down so that they convey little more than knowing facts. Trust, however, implies reliance, commitment, and confidence in the objects or truths that one is trusting. An element of commitment must be present in trusting Christ for salvation, but it is commitment to Him, His promise, and His ability to give eternal life to those who believe.

The object of faith or trust is the Lord Jesus Christ, however little or much one may know about Him. The issue about which we trust Him is His ability to forgive our sins and take us to heaven. And because He is the Lord God, there is an element in bowing before Him and acknowledging Him as a most superior person when one trusts Him for salvation.

BELIEF THAT DOES NOT SAVE

But is there not a kind of faith that does not save? Do not the demons exhibit such faith? In James 2:19 we are told that the demons believe and shudder. What is it that demons believe? The first part of the verse answers that question. They believe in one God. They are monotheists. And they shudder because they know that this God will someday judge them. They will not have the option of being judged by some other god who might overlook their sins, since there exists only one true God. James does not say what else they believe. In this verse, the only thing we are told is that they believe in one God. Thus this verse that is often quoted to show that some creatures can believe but not be saved is irrelevant to the issue of salvation, for it says only that demons are monotheists.

Nevertheless, it is true that some people can believe and not be saved. King Agrippa apparently believed the facts that confirmed that Jesus of Nazareth was the promised Savior (Acts 26:27). But he refused to receive Jesus and His salvation.

What makes the difference between those who believe and are not saved and those who believe and are saved? Apparently those who believe and are not saved know the facts of the Gospel and may even give assent to its truthfulness, but they are unwilling to trust the Savior for their personal salvation. Knowledge and assent without being willing to trust cannot in themselves save.

The New Testament always says that salvation is through faith, not because of faith (Ephesians 2:8). Faith is the channel through which we receive God's gift of forgiveness and eternal life. God has arranged it so that no one can ever boast, not even about his faith.

Normally the New Testament word for *believe* is used

with the preposition that means "in" (John 3:16), indicating reliance or confidence or trust in the object of the faith. Sometimes the word *believe* is followed by a preposition that means "upon," emphasizing laying hold on the object of faith (Romans 9:33). Sometimes it is followed by a clause that explains the content of faith (Romans 10:9, 11).

Does the New Testament use other words interchangeably with *believe?* Yes, it does. *Receive* is one (John 1:12); *call* is another (Romans 10:13). *Confess* is one (Romans 10:9; Hebrews 4:14); *ask* is another (John 4:10). *Come* is one (Revelation 22:17); *take* is another (Revelation 22:17). The person who asks or confesses or calls or receives or comes or takes, believes.

Of course, when one believes he commits to God. Commits what? His eternal destiny. That's the issue, not the years of his life on earth. Certainly when one believes he bows to a superior person, to the most superior person in all the universe. So superior that He can remove sin.

But it is not easy to believe that someone whom neither you nor any other living person has ever seen did something nearly two thousand years ago that can take away sin and make you acceptable before a holy God. But it is believing that brings eternal life.

NOTES

1. Charles Hodge, *Commentary on the Epistle to the Romans* (Grand Rapids: Eerdmans, 1967), 29.

2. Louis Berkhof, *Systematic Theology* (Grand Rapids: Eerdmans, 1941), 503–5.

3. Ibid., 505.

4. Ibid., 506.

5. John MacArthur, *The Gospel According to Jesus* (Grand Rapids: Zondervan, 1988), 173.

6. John Murray, *Redemption—Accomplished and Applied* (Grand Rapids: Eerdmans, 1965), 138.

By Him everyone who believes is justified from all things from which you could not be justified by the law of Moses.

Acts 13:39 NKJV

That [God] would be just and the justifier of the one who has faith in Jesus.

Romans 3:26

12

THE VERDICT: NOT GUILTY

Justification is one of those important words in the Scriptures that is either seldom defined or poorly defined. It simply means "to announce the verdict 'not guilty.'"

THE CONCEPT OF JUSTIFICATION

Justification does not make a person "not guilty"; it announces the fact that the individual is not guilty before God. Or to put the concept of "not guilty" positively, justification announces that the person is righteous before God. Again, it does not make the person righteous, but announces the fact that he is righteous.

As part of the Old Testament law for Israel, one of the provisions was this: "If there is a dispute between men and they go to court, . . . the judges decide their case, and they justify the righteous and condemn the wicked" (Deuteronomy 25:1). The judges did not make the person righteous or

wicked, nor could they. He was already righteous or wicked
when he appeared before the judges. What they did was examine the case and pronounce the verdict. They did not
change the person's character or actions; they announced a
verdict that they believed to be true and verified.

When King Solomon stood before his subjects at the
dedication of his temple, part of his prayer was this:

> If a man sins against his neighbor and is made to take an
> oath, and he comes and takes an oath before Your altar in
> this house, then hear in heaven and act and judge Your ser-
> vants, condemning the wicked by bringing his way on his
> own head and justifying the righteous by giving him accord-
> ing to his righteousness. (1 Kings 8:31–32)

Again it is quite clear that the person is righteous or
wicked before the verdict is rendered. The verdict does not
make him so; it announces what is so.

The courtroom, therefore, is the stage for the concept
of justification. When the judge justifies the person standing
before him, he announces that the person is not guilty of
whatever the charge was. In the courtroom of God, He announces not only that the sinner who has believed in Jesus is
not guilty, but that he is perfectly righteous before Him. Justification includes more than bare acquittal. The judge is not
only saying that the one standing before him may go without
penalty, but he also declares that as far as the law is concerned, the person is blameless and righteous.

GOD AS JUDGE

Throughout the Bible God is pictured as a judge (Genesis 18:25; 2 Timothy 4:8; James 5:9). Now if God, the
Judge, is without any injustice and completely righteous in
all His decisions, how can such a Judge announce a sinner
righteous? And sinners we all are. On what basis could He
possibly render a verdict of "not guilty" in the cases of sinners?

When a sinner stands before the bar of God, God only has three options with regard to his case. Either (1) He must condemn that sinner (and that would be perfectly just), (2) He must compromise His own holiness and find some sort of middle ground on which to accept him, or (3) He can change the sinner into a righteous person and then truly announce him as righteous. But such righteousness will have to be the kind that satisfies the standards of a holy God. It must be an actual righteousness, not a fictitious one. No sleight-of-hand tricks are allowed in that courtroom.

What God does is to put into effect the third option. He changes sinners into righteous people. How does He do that? By making us the righteousness of God in Christ (2 Corinthians 5:21), by making many righteous (Romans 5:19), by giving us the gift of righteousness (Romans 5:17). Who receives this gift of righteousness? The one "who has faith in Jesus" (Romans 3:26). Then what happens? God justifies him—announces him righteous in Christ. And at the same time God remains absolutely just (Romans 3:26).

Many misconceive justification as making us righteous rather than declaring us righteous. In other words, they think that our inward state of holiness, if enough, will cause God to rule in our favor. Our good works that make us righteous to one degree or another will result in some degree of justification. According to this misconception, justification can grow as we grow more righteous, and justification can be diminished and even lost if we become less righteous. Even though we acknowledge that God enables us to do good works, in the final analysis justification depends on us. And when would we know whether or not we had done enough good works to merit sufficient justification to gain heaven? How dedicated must I be in order to be justified? And for how long during my Christian life? Justification does not make anyone righteous; either we are or are not. And if we are, then God announces it so, and that is justification.

Notice Luke 7:29 (KJV): "And all the people that heard him, and the publicans, justified God." Obviously, the people did not make God righteous. They merely declared that He was, that He existed.

HOW CAN SINNERS BE RIGHTEOUS?

If justification does not make us righteous, what does? Also, if we cannot make ourselves righteous enough to satisfy a holy God, what hope is there that anyone can ever be justified? Will God have to condemn all people? Can He lower His standards enough to let some into heaven? Or is there some way He can change the sinner into a truly righteous person so that He can truly announce it so? As mentioned earlier, it is the latter course of action that He takes.

And how does God do that? By joining us to Jesus Christ when we believe. And because, then, we are in Christ, we have His perfect righteousness imputed to us; that is, placed on our account, so that we are in reality righteous in God's sight.

Impute is the key word. It means "to place to the account of." Perhaps the best illustration of imputation is the story told in the book of Philemon. Onesimus, the slave who ran away from his master Philemon in Colosse, found Paul and received Christ in Rome. At that point, Paul asked Onesimus to return to his master, assuring Philemon in a letter he sent along with the former slave that "if he [Onesimus] has wronged you in any way or owes you anything, charge that to my account" (Philemon 18). Likely this indicates that Onesimus had stolen property or money from Philemon when he ran away. In other words, Paul assured Philemon that he would pay whatever was necessary so that Onesimus need not be charged for anything he may have owed. Similarly, God imputes or puts on the believer's account the righteousness of Christ, so that in His sight we are completely righteous and He can announce it as so.

The logical, not chronological, procedure is this:

First, God devised a plan for providing the necessary righteousness in Jesus Christ. It was apart from law (Romans 3:21). In the Greek text, the word *law* appears without the article, indicating it was apart from not only the Mosaic Law that could not provide that righteousness (Acts 13:39) but also from all legal complications. That righteousness was manifested at the incarnation of Christ, having previously been predicted by the law and prophets of the Old Testament (1 Peter 1:10–11).

Second, righteousness comes through faith in the now-revealed Jesus (Romans 3:22).

Third, the price Christ had to pay in order that we might be righteous through faith was His own death (Romans 3:24–25). The cost to Him was surely the greatest.

Fourth, to us the benefit comes "as a gift" (verse 24), i.e., freely. The same word is translated "without a cause" in John 15:25; that is, without any cause in us. The gift of righteousness comes freely by His grace.

"Without any cause" in us rules out any requirement on our part except to have faith in His blood (that is, His atoning death). No requirement to commit to His mastery or even to be willing to do so can be found anywhere in this passage. When anyone believes in Jesus, he receives Christ's righteousness, and God can then announce that fact, which is justification. Even the way our Lord is designated in this passage does not inject any concept of Lord-Master. God justifies the one who "has faith in Jesus," and since the name *Jesus* means "God saves," then anyone who believes that Jesus (who is God) saves is justified.

THE GIFT OF RIGHTEOUSNESS

A companion passage, Romans 5:12–21, hammers home that this righteousness is a gift of grace. A gift is not a reward. Grace is not works. How difficult it is to comprehend grace, but the gift of righteousness comes by His grace to the one who does nothing other than believe in Jesus.

If a person would try to justify himself by his own works of righteousness, then his reward is not imputed according to the standard of grace but according to the standard of debt, "as what is due" (Romans 4:4). He is due a reward if works can justify, and God becomes obligated to him. Justification, under those circumstances, is no longer a gift of grace.

But, Paul continues, when one does not work but believes in God who justifies the ungodly, then his faith is imputed or reckoned for righteousness (Romans 4:5). Which will it be? Shall we work for righteousness and expect God to pay us with it? Or shall we not work at all for it and know that God will give the gift of righteousness to the one who believes in Jesus?

God's grace is unique among religions. One writer says:

> It is not found in any of the world's cults or religions, nor in much of what poses for Christianity. From the Pharisees' stress on deeds to the mystics' focus on meditation, all religions emphasize human achievement. They are all bilateral agreements: God does part, we do part. . . . But the God of Christianity is a God of unilateral action. . . . God acted on His own, making a unilateral declaration of grace.[1]

If God can remain just and announce a sinner righteous who believes in Jesus, how can anyone add anything else? If I can be justified by the judge of the universe through faith in Jesus, is any other requirement necessary? No. None. Did Paul leave out something? Was his message defective here because he did not inject the issue of lordship/mastery/commitment? No. Perish the thought.

JUSTIFICATION SHOWN

To be sure, justification is proved by personal purity. It does not come because of any reformation or commitment to change; but, once justified, we show this by changes in our lives. "He who has died is freed [literally, justified] from sin" (Romans 6:7). We stand acquitted from sin so that it no longer has dominion over us. Justification before the bar of God is demonstrated by changes in our lives here on earth before the bar of men.

THE VIEWPOINT OF JAMES

This was the perspective of the apostle James when he wrote that we are justified by works (James 2:24). Unproductive faith is a spurious faith; therefore, what we are in Christ will be seen in what we are before men. Men cannot peer into the courtroom of heaven to observe the Judge rendering a verdict of "not guilty" in respect to the sinner who believes. But men are spectators in the courtroom of life here on earth. When they see changed lives, they can know that there has been a heavenly verdict; that is, justification. When they do not see changes, then they may question and doubt. Justification by faith is necessary in the court of heaven. Justification by works is the only thing people can observe in the court on earth.

James gives an example of nonworking faith in the case of someone who sees a fellow believer in need of food and does not help meet that need (2:15–16). Faith that is not moved to relieve the hungry man's need is nonworking faith.

He offers two examples of saving, living, working faith in the lives of Abraham and Rahab. Abraham's faith and works of obedience are seen working together in his life. James 2:23 quotes Genesis 15:6, which clearly says that Abraham's faith was reckoned or imputed to him as righteousness without any added conditions. But that justifying faith was proved some thirty or more years later when Abraham showed the ultimate obedience in offering his son Isaac (Genesis 22, which James also cites in verse 21). By this act he proved beyond any doubt the reality of his Genesis 15 faith, which was at that point in his life reckoned to him as righteousness.

Similarly Rahab (James 2:25) evidenced her justification by her actions in helping the Israelite spies who canvassed Jericho (Joshua 2:1–21). Saving faith is a working faith, and those works justify believers in the courtroom on earth.

Justified in the sight of men. How? By faith that operates together with good works. Such saving faith is made complete, perfected, and carried to its end, since it finds fulfillment in good works (James 2:22).

Justified in the sight of the holy God? Yes. How? "Through faith in His blood." That gives me (not rewards me with) the gift of righteousness. That means God can be just and the justifier of "the one who has faith in Jesus." And it comes freely, without any cause in me, by His grace.

NOTE

1. Robert M. Horn, *Go Free* (Downers Grove, Ill.: InterVarsity, 1976), 42.

My sheep hear My voice, and I know them, and they follow Me; and I give eternal life to them, and they will never perish; and no one will snatch them out of My hand. My Father, who has given them to Me, is greater than all; and no one is able to snatch them out of the Father's hand.

John 10:27–29

For I am convinced that neither death, nor life, nor angels, nor principalities, nor things present, nor things to come, nor powers, nor height, nor depth, nor any other created thing, will be able to separate us from the love of God, which is in Christ Jesus our Lord.

Romans 8:38–39

13

SECURE AND SURE OF IT

Can a person lose his salvation, or is that salvation secure, able to endure until Christ returns? In answering this question, those who promote commitment or lordship salvation and those who do not, find agreement: a truly saved person cannot lose his or her salvation.

THE MEANING OF SECURITY

The belief that one cannot lose his or her salvation is called *eternal security.* What does eternal security mean? Let me propose a concise definition. Eternal security is that work of God which guarantees that the gift of salvation, once received, is possessed forever and cannot be lost. Since security rests on God's guarantee, its truthfulness does not rest on my feelings or experiences. Sometimes the teaching of eternal security is called the doctrine of preservation, which means that God preserves the believer in his salvation.

Some use the word *perseverance* or final perseverance to describe the concept of security or preservation. Perseverance emphasizes that the believer cannot finally or totally fall away from grace but will persevere to the end and be eternally saved. Perseverance seems to focus on the believer as the one who perseveres through the power of God. Security and preservation seem to focus on God as the one who secures our salvation. All acknowledge that although times of backsliding may come into the believer's life, fruit will be evident. Some who approach this doctrine from the emphasis of perseverance deny the possibility of a believer being carnal.

Although *security, preservation,* and *perseverance* essentially label the same doctrine, assurance is another matter, and differs from security. Assurance concerns the realization that a person has eternal life. But security is a true fact whether or not an individual has assurance of that.

But back to security. On what is this teaching based? Its basis is the grace of God who gives us the gift of eternal life, and that grace is eternal. Receiving that gift brings us into a relationship with all the persons of the Godhead, which guarantees and assures us that our salvation is eternally secure. Sometimes we cannot know for sure whether an individual is truly born again, but if he or she is, then that person's salvation is secure forever.

BELIEVING IN ETERNAL SECURITY: THE POWER OF THE FATHER AND THE SON

What are some of the specific reasons for believing in security? Consider these five, which rest on the power and purpose of the Father and the Son to keep us.

First, God the Father has purposed to glorify all those whom He predestined and called (Romans 8:30). *Predestined, called, justified,* and *glorified* are all written in the same tense in this verse, indicating that the glorification of all believers is as certain as their predestination, calling, and justification. And remember, we are justified through faith in Jesus, not faith *and* commitment of life (Romans 3:26).

Second, although most would agree that God's power is fully able to keep the believer secure (Jude 24), some argue that His power can be cut off if a person renounces his faith. But *the Lord said that we are secure in His and the Father's hand, and that guarantees that He will keep safe the one who has received the gift of eternal life* (John 10:28–29). No one (including ourselves) is able to snatch us out of God's hand. And remember, eternal life is a gift received through faith, not a reward for being willing to follow Christ.

Third, our Lord's continual intercession for us keeps us saved completely and eternally (Hebrews 7:25). When we do sin, we have our Lord to plead our case before God (1 John 2:1–2). And because He has provided total and eternal satisfaction or propitiation for our sins, we stand forgiven. Satan accuses us (Revelation 12:10), and often we accuse ourselves, but with Christ defending us on the basis of His death for our sins, nothing can undo the great salvation which we have received.

"Who will bring a charge against God's elect?" Paul asks (Romans 8:33). It makes no difference what the answer is. It makes no difference who in all the universe may try to charge us with whatever. It makes no difference as long as it is not God who charges us. And God does not. In fact, He has already announced the verdict in all instances when we are and will be charged. And that verdict is "not guilty." Paul answers his own question about who will charge God's elect by simply saying, "God is the one who justifies" (verse 33). Every single time we sin, a charge can be legitimately leveled at us. But whenever that happens, whoever brings the accusation finds that the case has already been decided and the verdict rendered, "Not guilty."

Fourth, nothing and no one (including ourselves) can separate us from the everlasting love of God (Romans 8:35–39). In this passage, Paul lists a number of candidates that might seem to be able to separate believers from the love of Christ. They include, among others: adverse circumstances like trouble and poverty; all the circumstances of life, present and future, including death; and the powers of angelic beings (and Satan is one of them). Then Paul concludes by saying no other created thing can separate us from the love of God in Christ. Nothing in all creation, including all the creatures (which includes us), can cause a separation from the eternal love of Christ.

Fifth, if our salvation is not secure, then our new birth would have to be able to die or we would have to be able to destroy it by some act of sin. But never does the New Testament even hint that such could happen. Regeneration is that work of God that gives to the one who believes new life through the new birth. Further, regeneration is instantaneous—either one is dead in sin or alive in Christ. A process may be involved that leads to the new birth, but the birth occurs at a given moment of time.

And how is a person regenerated?

> God does it (John 1:13)
>> according to His will (James 1:18)
>> through the Holy Spirit (John 3:5)
>>> and the washing of regeneration (Titus 3:5)
>>> when a person believes (John 1:12)
>>>> the Gospel revealed in the Word (1 Peter 1:23).

And remember, John 1:12 states clearly that receiving Christ—that is, believing on His name—makes one a child of God. To be sure, the new birth will result in a changed lifestyle, but we become children of God through faith.

REASONS FOR BELIEVING IN ETERNAL SECURITY: THE WORK OF THE HOLY SPIRIT

The work of the Holy Spirit gives us additional reasons to believe in the eternal security of our salvation. Consider these three works of the Spirit and their implications for our eternal security.

First, the abiding presence and residence of the Holy Spirit in the believer is also a gift from God (John 7:37–39; Acts

SECURE AND SURE OF IT

11:16–17; Romans 5:5; 1 Corinthians 2:12). If salvation can be lost, then God would have to take back His gift of the Spirit.

Second, at conversion the believer is joined to the body of Christ by the baptism of the Holy Spirit (1 Corinthians 12:13). If salvation can be lost, then one would have to be severed from the body, and the body of Christ would then be dismembered.

Third, when we believed, the Holy Spirit sealed us until the day of redemption (Ephesians 1:13; 4:30). If we are not secure, then the seal has to be broken or the promise would be that we are sealed not until the day of redemption but only until the day we sin (or at least commit some very serious or grievous sin). And remember, God seals *all* believers, not just those who are, or who are willing to be, committed believers (2 Corinthians 1:22).

THE TESTIMONY OF THE
APOSTLE PAUL IN 2 TIMOTHY 2:11–13

One other reason causes us to believe our salvation is secure. The apostle Paul cited in 2 Timothy 2:11–13 what was apparently part of an early Christian hymn in New Testament times. That hymn and Paul's endorsement of it in the Scriptures give strong assurance of the believer's security. Paul wrote that "it is a trustworthy statement."

Four couplets are recorded, two positive and two negative. The first is, "If we died with Him, we will also live with Him"—likely a reference to our co-crucifixion with Christ (as explained in Romans 6:1–10).

The second is, "If we endure, we will also reign with Him." Here the contrast is between the endurance necessary in this life and the ultimate glorification which all believers will enjoy (Romans 8:17).

The third couplet, "If we deny Him, he also will deny us," reiterates the Lord's word in Matthew 10:33. Judas did this. The last couplet, however, assures us that "if we are faithless, He remains faithful; for He cannot deny Himself."

This is no warning of certain condemnation to false profes-sors; rather "Christ's constancy to His own promises pro-vides the believer with his greatest security. It is unthinkable that any contingency could affect the faithfulness of God, for he cannot deny himself."[1] "He will not deny even unprofitable members of His own body. True children of God cannot be-come something other than children, even when disobedient and weak. Christ's faithfulness to Christians is not contin-gent on their faithfulness to Him."[2]

Could being "faithless" include unbelief? Could a true believer disbelieve and still be saved? Charles J. Ellicott, Greek scholar of the last century, while acknowledging the possibility of the translation "faithless," said that the word means

> "If we exhibit unbelief," whether as regards His attributes, His promises, or His Gospel . . . nor here is there sufficient reason for departing from the regular meaning of *apistein* [to disbelieve] (Mark xvi. 11, 41, Acts xxviii. 24), which, like *apistia* [unbelief], seems always in the N.T. to imply not "un-trueness," "unfaithfulness," but definitely "unbelief."[3]

Normally one who has believed can be described as a believer; that is, one who continues to believe. But according to Ellicott, apparently a believer may come to the place of not believing, and yet God will not disown him, since He cannot disown Himself.

Some years ago a book by Robert Shank, entitled *Life in the Son,*[4] argued against eternal security on the basis that the uses of *believe* in the present tense in the New Testament show that if a believer did not continue to believe he could and would lose his salvation. Today proponents of lordship/discipleship/mastery salvation use the same argument to conclude that if someone does not continue to believe, then he or she was never a believer in the first place.[5] However, notice that when Abraham's faith is described in the New Testament, an aorist, not a present, tense is used consistently

(Romans 4:3; Galatians 3:6; James 2:23). Many Samaritans believed (aorist) the harlot's testimony and were saved (John 4:39, 41). Others believed (aorist) (John 10:42; 11:45; Acts 14:1; 1 Corinthians 15:11). And in response to the Philippian jailer's question, Paul said, "Believe" (aorist, Acts 16:31).

As Lenski wrote in his commentary on Acts:

> *Pisteuson* [believe] is properly the aorist, for the moment one believes, salvation is his. "To believe" always means to put all trust and confidence in the Lord Jesus, in other words, by such trust of the heart to throw the personality entirely into his arms for deliverance from sin, death, and hell. Here *epi* [on or upon] is used; this trust is to rest on Jesus. . . . To trust him is to let him give us that salvation. . . . To believe is to accept the divine gift of salvation and at once to have it.[6]

THE MEANING OF ASSURANCE

Assurance is a different matter. Assurance is the confident realization that one has eternal life. Security is a biblical truth whether or not one has assurance, and even if one did not believe in security he could have assurance (that at that time, at least, he belonged to the family of God). But if one does not believe in security he will undoubtedly lack assurance more than once in his lifetime.

SOME REASONS PEOPLE LACK ASSURANCE

People lack assurance of their salvation for several reasons:

1. They cannot pinpoint a specific time when they received Christ. Conversion does occur at a specific time, yet a person may not know when that time was in his or her life. No one grows into conversion, but we do grow in our comprehension of conversion.
2. They question the correctness of the procedure they went through when they expressed faith in Christ. "Should I have 'gone forward'?" "Did I pray the right prayer?" "I did it privately. Is that all right?"

3. Certain sins have come into their lives. They think that they surely were not saved in the first place or they would not have committed such sins. Security never gives a license to sin, but at the same time sin does not cause us to lose our salvation. The normal Christian experience never includes sinlessness, for "we all stumble in many ways" (James 3:2). This fact never excuses sin, but neither does sin cause us to forfeit our salvation.

HOW TO BE ASSURED YOU ARE SAVED

How can I have assurance? The Bible offers two grounds for assurance. The objective ground is that God's Word declares that I am saved through faith. Therefore, I believe Him and His Word and am assured that what He says is true (John 5:24; 1 John 5:1, 13).

The subjective ground relates to my experiences. Certain changes do accompany salvation, and when I see some of those changes, then I can be assured that I have received new life. Some of those changes are keeping His commandments (1 John 2:3); loving other believers (1 John 2:9–11; 3:14); and doing right things (1 John 2:29; 3:9). It goes without saying that I will never keep all His commandments, nor will I love all other believers, nor will I always do right things. But the fact that these experiences have come into my life, whereas they were absent before, gives assurance that the new life is present (2 Corinthians 5:17).

If we have believed, we are secure forever; and we can be assured of that if we take God at His Word and take heart from the changes which He brings into our lives.

What grace it is that can give us not only forgiveness and eternal life through faith alone but also guarantee that the Giver will never renege on His gift! Nor can we ever give it back even if we try! Be assured, fellow Christian, this is true, for God says so in His unbreakable Word.

NOTES

1. Donald Guthrie, *The Pastoral Epistles* (Grand Rapids: Eerdmans, 1957), 146.

2. A. Duane Litfin, "2 Timothy," vol. 1 *The Bible Knowledge Commentary* (Wheaton, Ill.: Victor, 1983), 1:748.

3. Charles J. Ellicott, *The Pastoral Epistles of St. Paul* (London: Longman, 1864), 130.

4. Robert Shank, *Life in the Son* (Springfield, Mo.: Westcott, 1960).

5. John MacArthur, *The Gospel According to Jesus* (Grand Rapids: Zondervan, 1988), 172.

6. R. C. H. Lenski, *The Acts of the Apostles* (Columbus, Ohio: Wartburg, 1947), 680–81.

Now to Him who is able to keep you from stumbling, and to make you stand in the presence of His glory blameless with great joy, to the only God our Savior, through Jesus Christ our Lord, be glory, majesty, dominion and authority, before all time and now and forever.

Jude 24–25

14

BRINGING MANY SONS TO GLORY

I once kept an account at a bank that offered what they called "The Grand Plan." Those bank customers who kept a certain amount of money on deposit could qualify for the Grand Plan, which offered a number of free benefits. As a matter of fact, Grand Plan customers received checks with a Grand Plan logo printed on them so that any teller could see immediately that you belonged to that special group. It was a good deal for those who could qualify.

God has the ultimate Grand Plan. To qualify requires only faith in Christ as one's Savior. Then the benefits become available immediately and continue forever. His Grand Plan began in eternity past and continues throughout eternity future. Its purpose is to bring or lead many sons to glory (Hebrews 2:10).

THE LAMB PROVIDED

The roots of God's plan of redemption existed before the foundation of the world (1 Peter 1:19–20). Even before man was created, the Lamb was provided. Certainly before man sinned in the Garden of Eden, the Lamb had already been provided. God did not have to scurry around seeing what plan He could come up with when Adam and Eve rebelled against Him. The Lamb, without spot or blemish, had already been provided in the purpose and Grand Plan of God.

In the fullness of time God sent the Lamb (Galatians 4:4; Titus 2:11). He lived a sinless life and thus proved to be spotless and fully qualified as the acceptable sacrifice for sin. He died, and by that death He paid for the sins of the whole world, although the personal appropriation of that payment comes through faith. He reconciled the world to Himself, yet to make that applicable to me personally, I have to be reconciled to God through faith (2 Corinthians 5:19–20).

THE PEOPLE CHOSEN

God also chose a people before the foundation of the world who would be the "many sons" He would eventually bring to glory (Ephesians 1:1–14). Election is a biblical teaching, albeit not an easy one. When the apostle Paul approaches the subject it is with a wonder and amazement that God could and would choose anyone. If God could not or did not elect, none would be saved, for all have sinned and no one seeks God (Romans 5:12; 3:11). If Almighty God could not have retreated into His sovereignty to choose a people He would bring to glory, then no one could ever hope to be saved. "So then it does not depend on the man who wills or the man who runs, but on God who has mercy" (Romans 9:16).

The time of God's choosing is expressly stated to have been before the foundation of the world (Ephesians 1:4). The basis of the choice is God's own good pleasure, not man's works (verses 5, 11). His purpose, His good pleasure, and His will are all involved in that choosing. God's purpose is to glorify Himself (verse 12). In this fact (though we cannot fully understand it) lies the resolution of all the problems and questions concerning God's elective purpose. He, whose attributes never war against each other but are always in harmony, glorifies Himself. That means that the God who is love, and the God who is light, and the God who is holy, and the God who is just, and the God who is merciful is the God who chose and the God who is glorified by that choosing. Election, though unfathomable to the human mind, need not be uncomfortable to the human heart, since it is our gracious, loving God who did it.

THE PEOPLE ADOPTED

Part of God's Grand Plan includes being predestined to the adoption as sons (Ephesians 1:5). When God adopts, He places the believer in His family as a fully privileged adult. Adoption (a Pauline doctrine) makes us adults in God's family; the new birth (a Johannine doctrine) causes us to be born as babes in God's family. Adoption includes and guarantees full standing and privileges in the family. Being born into the family brings with it the need for growth and development and maturity. Being adopted and being born both occur simultaneously at the moment one receives the Savior.

Adoption cuts off all the relationships and responsibilities of the former family. At the same time, God, the head of the new family, has promised never to cut off those whom He adopts. Therefore, adoption assures us that all the adopted sons will be brought to glory.

Many early cultures practiced something akin to adoption. Moses, a slave, was adopted by Pharaoh's daughter in Egypt. Ancient tablets record a custom whereby a childless couple could adopt a son who would be their heir. Hebrew laws did not include a law about adoption, probably because there was a law that provided that if a man who died had an

eligible brother, the brother would marry his widowed sister-
in-law and have children who would inherit the family name
and property.

Adoption was common in Greek and Roman life.
Childless couples would often adopt a son who would then
become their heir. Even if the adopted son had living biolog-
ical parents, they had no more claim over him after the adoption took place. Parents were often willing to let their sons be
adopted by another family, especially if it meant a better life
for their son.

Paul says that God predestined for adoption into His
family all those whom He chose (Ephesians 1:5). God's Grand
Plan included our being destined to be placed as fully privileged sons in the family of God. This is made possible by the
death of Christ (Galatians 4:5), and we actually become
adult sons "through faith in Christ Jesus" (Galatians 3:26).
In these passages, subjective, personal lordship is no issue or
condition. Adoption happens through faith in Christ Jesus.
We received adoption; we do not earn it. And we are assured
of it because of the presence of the Holy Spirit in our lives
(Galatians 4:5–6).

The group that was chosen before the foundation of
the world is the same group that receives adoption through
faith, the same group that God pronounces "not guilty," and
the same group of sons who will come to glory. Indeed, Paul
is so bold as to write that this group is already glorified (Romans 8:30). It is so certain that not one will slip away from
the group, that those whom He predestined He has glorified.
Saints go to a guaranteed glory. What grace it is that can ac-
complish God's Grand Plan!

THE FACETS OF SANCTIFICATION

But what of sanctification? Nowhere does it appear in
Paul's list in Romans 8:29–30. Only predestination, calling,
justification, and glorification. Why is sanctification not included? Could it be that Paul did not want to base our guarantee of ultimate glorification on our personal sanctification?

Assuredly it does not rest on that, for the many sons who will be glorified will have exhibited varying degrees of personal holiness during their lifetimes. Yet all, from the carnal to the most mature, will be glorified.

Some of the confusion may arise from a failure to distinguish the facets of sanctification. The word *sanctify* basically means "to set apart." It has the same root as the words *holy* and *saint*. Every believer has been sanctified, for all have been set apart to God and adopted into His family. That is why all believers are saints. Even of the carnal Christians at Corinth, Paul dared to say that they were washed, they were sanctified, and they were justified (1 Corinthians 6:11). The same tense (indicating an accomplished fact, not something to be attained) is used for all three verbs. This aspect of sanctification separates all believers to their new position as belonging to God. Paul had already addressed these Corinthians as those who had been sanctified (1 Corinthians 1:2; notice also his use of the same verb and tense in Acts 20:32 and 26:18). Positional sanctification is an actual position that is not dependent on the state of one's spiritual growth and maturity. The one-time offering of our Lord Jesus has sanctified us and perfected us in perpetuity—forever (Hebrews 10:10, 14).

But quite obviously all believers do not evidence this position in their practices. Sanctification therefore has a second aspect that relates to the progressive work of continuing to be set apart during one's entire Christian life. Every biblical exhortation to godly living underscores this aspect of sanctification (1 Peter 1:16).

But there is also a third facet of sanctification that awaits the believer's glorification with his resurrection body and removal of the sin nature (1 John 3:1–3; Jude 24). When we are ultimately set apart of God in heaven, then our position and our practice will be in perfect accord.

Both dispensational and Reformed writers recognize these three aspects of sanctification.

To capsulize these three aspects of sanctification, one

might say this: Sanctified people (by position) need to be sanctified (in practice), and they will be sanctified (ultimately).

JUSTIFICATION AND SANCTIFICATION

What is the relationship between justification and sanctification? Both Reformed and dispensational theologians believe that both positional sanctification and justification occur simultaneously at the time of salvation. John Murray, a Reformed theologian, states clearly that "the virtue accruing from the death and resurrection of Christ affects no phase of salvation more directly than that of insuring definitive sanctification."[1] He also clearly distinguishes positional (or definitive) sanctification and progressive sanctification. "It might appear that the emphasis placed upon definitive sanctification leaves no place for what is progressive. Any such inference would contradict an equally important aspect of biblical teaching."[2]

THE PEOPLE DISCIPLINED

In His Grand Plan to bring many sons to glory, the Father will discipline His children (Hebrews 12:5–11). Four reasons are stated by the writer of Hebrews that tell why God does this:

1. Discipline is a part of the total educational process by which a believer is fitted to share God's holiness (verse 10).
2. Discipline is a proof of a genuine love relationship between our heavenly Father and us (verses 6, 8).
3. Discipline helps train us to be obedient (verse 9).
4. Discipline produces the fruit of righteousness in our lives (verse 11).

MEANS FOR PROGRESSIVE SANCTIFICATION

Who and what are the agencies involved in progressive sanctification? Our Father is one (John 17:17; 15:2). Our Lord Jesus is another (John 17:15; Ephesians 5:26–27). The Holy Spirit is another (2 Corinthians 3:18). The believer's efforts are not optional. God's part in sanctification must never lead to a quietism that fails to involve the believer's activity (Romans 6:19; 2 Corinthians 7:1; Galatians 5:16). Indeed, every command to the believer implies the necessity of his involvement as part of the process. Some verses combine the believer's part and God's part in the process of sanctification (Romans 8:13; Philippians 2:13; Colossians 1:29).

In addition, certain means or things can be used both by God and by the believer to help this growth in holiness. Surely the Word of God stands in the first rank of importance (John 17:17). Certainly prayer will aid the process, if praying is done truly in the name of Christ. That simply means praying so that the Lord could endorse those prayers, or praying in His will. It means underscoring all our prayers with, as Jesus' own model prayer instructs us, "Your will be done, on earth as it is in heaven" (Matthew 6:10).

Actually, every circumstance of life can be reacted to so as to further or hinder the process of sanctification. God can make all things work together for good to those who love Him (Romans 8:28), and we can in everything give thanks, knowing that this is God's will for us (1 Thessalonians 5:18). We could well pray every day that our reactions to the events of that day will be such as to draw us closer to our Lord and never away from Him.

God's Grand Plan started with the provision of a Savior. It involved choosing a people. It gave us the Savior at a point in time and history. It led us to receive the gift of eternal life at some point in the history of our lives. It gave us the position as adopted sons in the family of God. It sanctified us forever. It disciplines us and leads us in paths of righteousness during our lives here on earth. And someday it will be consummated by conforming us to the image of Christ. This is what we have been destined for, and the exact same group that was so destined will be brought to glory (Romans 8:29–30; Hebrews 2:10). To be perfectly and fully conformed to the image of Christ will someday be our joy. In the meantime it is our job to be so, even though never perfectly and fully.

Free? Yes.

Cheap? Never.

It's grace all the way. It's grace that establishes and perfects us: "After you have suffered for a little while, the God of all grace, who called you to His eternal glory in Christ, will Himself perfect, confirm, strengthen and establish you. To Him be dominion forever and ever" (1 Peter 5:10–11).

> O the love that drew salvation's plan!
> O the grace that bro't it down to man!
> O the mighty gulf that God did span
> At Calvary!
>
> Mercy there was great, and grace was free,
> Pardon there was multiplied to me,
> There my burdened soul found liberty—
> At Calvary.

William R. Newell

NOTES

1. John Murray, "Sanctification (the Law)," *Basic Christian Doctrines*, ed. by Carl F. H. Henry (New York: Holt, Rinehart & Winston, 1962), 229.

2. Ibid.

DEFINITIONS OF
KEY TERMS

Abiding in Christ. To live in harmony with the Lord by keeping His commandments.

Adoption. To be placed in God's family as an adult with all privileges of that position.

Assurance of salvation. The realization or confidence that through faith in Christ one truly possesses eternal life.

Believe. To hold something as true.

Carnal. To have the characteristics of an unsaved life either because one is an unbeliever or because, though a believer, one is living like an unsaved person.

Dedication. The act of presenting oneself to God for His control and use.

Disciple. A follower of a teacher and his teachings, involving, in Bible times, traveling with that teacher wherever he went.

Discipline. Training that molds the believer toward Christlikeness.

Easy believism. The idea that to give mere assent to the facts of the Gospel is too easy and cannot save unless a commitment to submit one's life is made at the same time.

Election. God's choice before time of those who would be saved.

Eternal security. The work of God which guarantees that the gift of God (salvation), once received, is possessed forever and cannot be lost.

Faith. Being convinced or giving credence to something or someone, especially to the truth of the Gospel.

Fruit. In the New Testament, fruit is Christlikeness, good works, witnessing, praising, and giving.

Glorify God. God is glorified when any of His characteristics are seen.

Gospel. Good story or good news, especially about the death and resurrection of Christ as payment for believers' sin.

Grace. The unmerited favor of God in giving His Son and all the benefits that result from receiving Him.

Impute. To reckon or ascribe something to someone; e.g., God's ascribing the righteousness of Christ to the believer.

Justification. To declare a person righteous. God does this for the believer because He has imputed the righteousness of

Christ to that person. People justify others when they see their good works.

Lord. A superior. In the New Testament, it means sir, sovereign, master, God, owner, and husband.

Lordship salvation. The teaching that to be saved a person must not only trust Jesus as Savior but also as the Lord of his life, submitting (or at least being willing to submit) his life to His sovereign authority.

Perseverance. The belief that a believer cannot fall away from grace but will continue in good works to the end of life.

Predestination. God's planning before time the destiny of His children to be conformed to the image of Christ.

Propitiation. The turning away of God's wrath because of the offering of Christ on the cross.

Pruning. Removing useless things, both good and bad, from the believer's life so that he or she can be more fruitful.

Redemption. To be liberated because a price has been paid. Christ's death liberated believers from the penalty and power of sin.

Regeneration. God giving new life by the new birth to the one who believes in Jesus.

Repentance. A change of mind about something or someone in a way that effects some change in the individual.

Salvation. God's deliverance for the believer from all the effects of sin, plus all the benefits which He bestows now and forever.

Sanctification. God setting the believer apart for Himself: positionally at salvation, progressively throughout life, and ultimately when the believer arrives in His presence in heaven.

SCRIPTURE INDEX

Genesis		21:8	99–100
13:11	102	21:9	100
15:6	121	25:1–3	99
18:25	116		
19:5–8	101	Deuteronomy	
19:14	102	6:5	76
19:16	102	25:1	115
22:21	121		
		Joshua	
Exodus		2:1–21	121
20:3	76		
		1 Samuel	
Leviticus		17:42	100
19:18	76		
		1 Kings	
Numbers		8:31–32	116
21:4–9	99		

Psalms		1:14–15	37
16:8–11	85	2:28	64
74:20	100	8:35	37
94:9	100	10:17–31	74
110	86	10:21	76, 78
119:6	100	10:25	78
119:15	100	10:29	37
		13:10	37
Isaiah		14:9	37
5:12	100	16:11	130
		16:15	37
Matthew		16:41	130
2:8	94		
3:1–2	36	Luke	
4:17	36	2:10	37
6:10	141	4:43	37
7:13–14	22	6:17	94
8:6	64	7:29	117
9:12	90	9:23	21
9:14	94	9:61	70
10:1	95	14:16–33	69–71
10:5–7	36	14:25–33	95
10:33	129	14:26	77
13:8	50, 53	14:33	76
13:44	82	15:10	42
17:1	95	18:18–30	74
18:24	78	18:25	78
19:16–30	74	19:10	90
21:28–32	84	19:11	37
22:16	94	19:33	64
24:14	37	19:37–39	94
26:13	37	23:50	96
26:63–66	66	24:46–47	87
28:18–20	93		
		John	
Mark		1:1–18	98
1:1	37	1:12	113, 128

1:13	128	Acts		
1:29	47	2:22–31	85–86
3:1–21	37	2:34	86
3:5	128	2:36	65, 86
3:12	88	2:38	85, 87
3:14	99	2:39	86
3:15	88	3:19	65
3:16	78, 98, 113	4:12	82
4:10	88, 101, 113	5:31	87
4:11	64	9:25	94
4:18	101	10:14	67
4:26	101	11:16–17	128–29
4:39	88, 131	11:18	87
4:41	131	13:39	75, 119
4:41–42	88	14:1	131
5:8	47	16:18	139
5:24	100, 132	16:31	87, 96–98,
6:40	100		110, 131
6:66	77, 94	17:30–31	88
7:37–39	128	19:1–20	102
8:31	94	19:18	102
10:24	66	20:21	88–89
10:28–29	127	20:32	139
10:30	66	22:10	68
10:33	66	26:27	112
10:42	131	28:24	130
11:45	131		
13:13–16	64	Romans	
15:1–17	47–50	1:13	46
15:2	140	3:11	136
15:25	119	3:20	75
17:15	140	3:21	118
17:17	140, 141	3:22	119
19:38	94, 95	3:24–25	119
20:28	64	3:26	117, 126
20:31	24, 88	4:3	131
		4:4	119

4:5	87, 120	2:12	129
4:25	38, 110	3:1–3	29
5:5	129	3:1–4	55–58
5:12	136	3:12	58
5:12–21	119	3:15	49
5:17	117	4:5	42, 58
5:19	117	6:11	56, 139
6:1–10	129	6:19–20	68
6:3	68	8:5	64
6:6	87	12:3	65, 66, 67, 86
6:7	120	12:13	129
6:13	68	15:3–4	24, 28, 110
6:19	141	15:3–8	37–38
7:18	54	15:11	131
7:25	54	15:39	54
8:5–8	55	16:15	46
8:9	55		
8:13	141	**2 Corinthians**	
8:17	129	1:22	129
8:28	141	3:18	140
8:29–30	138, 141	5:17	132
8:30	126	5:19–20	136
8:33	127	5:21	117
8:35–39	127–28	7:1	141
9:16	136	7:9–11	89
9:33	113	10:4	54
10:9	86, 113	12:7–10	48
10:9–10	65–67		
10:11	113	**Galatians**	
10:13	113	1:6	36
12:1	68	3:6	131
15:27	54	3:26	138
15:28	46	4:4	136
		4:5–6	138
1 Corinthians		5:16	141
1:2	139	5:17	58
1:12	57	5:19–24	54

5:22–23	46	Titus	
		2:11	136
Ephesians		3:5	128
1:1–14	136	3:14	41
1:4	136		
1:5	137, 138	Philemon	
1:11	137	18	118
1:12	137		
1:13	129	Hebrews	
2:3	54	2:10	135, 141
2:8	65, 112	4:14	113
2:8–9	87	5:7	54
4:28	59	5:11–6:2	57
4:30	129	7:25	127
4:32	14	10:10	139
5:26–27	140	10:14	139
		10:34	48
Philippians		12:5–11	48, 140
1:19	82	12:17	85
1:22	46	13:15	46
2:11	65		
2:13	141	James	
4:17	46	1:18	128
		1:27	48
Colossians		2:15–16	121
1:10	46	2:19	109, 112
1:29	141	2:22	122
		2:23	121, 131
1 Thessalonians		2:24	121
3:6	36	2:25	121
5:18	141	3:2	59, 132
		4:7	68
2 Timothy		4:7–10	21
2:11–13	129–31	5:9	116
2:25	89		
4:8	116		

1 Peter		2:9–11	132
1:2	58	2:16	54
1:10–11	119	2:19	78
1:16	139	2:29	132
1:19–20	136	3:1–3	139
1:23	128	3:9	132
3:6	64	3:14	132
4:12–16	48	3:24	49
4:14	59	4:3	66
4:15	59	5:1	132
4:16	59	5:13	132
5:10–11	142		
5:12	59	2 John	
		8	49
2 Peter			
1:5–7	50	Jude	
1:5–8	46	24	127, 139
1:8	41		
2:1	82	Revelation	
2:7	102	2:5	89
3:9	87	2:21–22	89
		3:3	89
1 John		3:19	89
2:1–2	127	12:10	127
2:3	132	22:17	113

SUBJECT INDEX

Abiding in Christ, 48–50
Adoption, 137–38
Assent, intellectual, 28–29
Assurance, 126, 131–32

Baptism (Spirit), 38, 129
Baptism (water), 16, 23, 31, 93–94
Bavinck, Herman, 56
Belief/believing
    difficulty of, 107–8
    faithlessness and, 130–31
    New Testament usage of term, 112–13
    See also Faith
Berkhof, Louis, 110–11

Bible, 21
Bruce, F. F., 86

Calvin, John, 31, 56
Carnality
    in believers, 55–56
    evidences of, 29, 56–58
    meaning of, 54
    misconceptions about, 29–30, 53–54
    newness of teaching on, 30–31
    seriousness of, 58–59
Christlikeness, 46
Clark, Gordon, 20–21
Commandments, 75–76

Deathbed conversions, 42–
    43, 94
Decisional salvation, 28–29
Dedication, 67–68
Demons, 109, 112
Discipleship
    cost of, 70
    eternal life and, 77–78
    lordship and, 96–98
    types of, 94–96
Discipline, 140

Election, 136–37
Ellicott, Charles J., 130
Ephesian believers, 102–3
Eternal security
    constancy of Christ and,
        129–30
    meaning of, 125–26
    Holy Spirit and, 128–29
    power and purpose of
        God and, 126–28

Faith
    and lordship gospel, 28–
        29, 43–45, 99
    and repentance, 81–82,
        86, 87–89, 90
    meaning of, 28, 109–11
    nonsaving, 112
    three aspects of, 110–11
    See also Belief/believing
Faithlessness, 130–31
Flesh and fleshly, 54
Forgiveness, 38–39

Fruit and fruitfulness
    abiding and, 48–50
    deathbed conversions
        and, 42–43
    defined, 45–47
    lordship view of, 43–45
    necessity of, 41–42
    pruning and, 47–48
Full Gospel, 38

Gentry, K. L., 97
Giving, 46
Giving one's heart to Christ,
    24
Glorification, 138
God, as judge, 116–17
Gospel
    direction of, 39
    expressions of, 21–24
    meaning of, 37–38
    of the kingdom, 36–37
    semantics and, 23–24
    types of, 36–37
Grace
    cost of, 16
    difficulty of believing in,
        16
    effect of, 17
    meaning of, 15–16
    uniqueness of, 120
Great Commission, 87,
    93–94

Harrison, Everett, 65–66
Hodge, Charles, 110, 111
Holy Spirit, 30, 38, 128–29

Imputation, 118
Inerrancy, 21
Intellectual assent, 28–29

Jesus Christ
  as Lord, 64–67, 86
  as Lord of life, 67–68
  love of, 78
Joseph of Arimathea, 95–96
Josephus, 84
Justification
  demonstration of, 120–22
  meaning of, 115–16, 117–18
  righteousness and, 118–20
  sanctification and, 140

Language, purpose of, 20–21
Law, 74–76
Lenski, R. C. H., 131
Lightfoot, J. B., 56, 57
Lord
  Jesus Christ as, 64–67, 86
  meanings of, 63–64
Lordship salvation
  discipleship in, 96–98
  fruitfulness in, 43–45
  repentance in, 87
  willingness in, 76–77
Lot, 101–2

MacArthur, John, 33, 50, 60, 79, 104, 113, 133
Messiah, 96–97, 98

Millennial kingdom, 37
Murray, John, 111

Obedience, 49

Perseverance, 126
Pink, Arthur W., 98
Possessions, 76–77, 78–79
Praise, 46
Prayer, 49, 141
Premillennialism, 31
Pruning, 47–48

Quotations, use of, 31–32

Ransom-to-Satan theory, 31
Redemption, 82
Regeneration, 128, 137
Repentance
  of Christians, 89, 90
  lordship view of, 87
  meaning of, 82–83
  necessity of, 23–24
  New Testament usage of term, 83–89
  nonsaving, 83–85
  saving, 85–89
Righteousness, 118–20
Ryle, J. C., 59–60

Salvation
  freeness of, 69–70
  meaning of, 82
  provision of, 136
  requirements for, 98–100
Samaritan woman, 101

Sanctification
    facets of, 138–40
    justification and, 140
    means of, 140–41
Semantics, 19–20, 21
Shedd, William G. T., 66
Sin
    forgiveness of, 38–39
    sorrow for, 81, 82–83, 85,
        90
Surrender, 16

Trench, R. C., 84
Trust, 110, 111–12

Uncommitted believers,
    101–3

Westcott, B. F., 66
Whole Gospel, 38
Witness, 46
Works, 16–17, 23, 46